Separate Agendas

Separate Agendas

Churchill, Eisenhower, and Anglo-American Relations, 1953–1955

Daniel C. Williamson

LEXINGTON BOOKS

A division of
ROWMAN & LITTLEFIELD PUBLISHERS, INC.
Lanham • Boulder • New York • Toronto • Plymouth, UK

LEXINGTON BOOKS

A division of Rowman & Littlefield Publishers, Inc.
A wholly owned subsidiary of The Rowman & Littlefield Publishing Group, Inc.
4501 Forbes Boulevard, Suite 200
Lanham, MD 20706

Estover Road
Plymouth PL6 7PY
United Kingdom

First paperback edition 2007

British Library Cataloguing in Publication Information Available

The hardback edition of this book was previously cataloged by the Library of Congress as follows:
Williamson, Daniel C., 1963–
Separate agendas : Churchill, Eisenhower, and Anglo-American relations, 1953–1955 / Daniel C. Williamson.
p. cm.
Includes bibliographical references and index.
ISBN 0-7391-1164-7 (cloth : alk. paper)
1. United States—Foreign relations—Great Britain. 2. Great Britain—Foreign relations—United States. 3. United States—Foreign relations—1953–1961. 4. Churchill, Winston, Sir, 1874–1965. 5. Eisenhower, Dwight D. (Dwight David), 1890–1969. 6. World politics—1945–1955. 7. Middle East—Politics and government—1945–1979. 8. East Asia—Politics and government—20th century. 9. Europe—Politics and government—1945– I. Title.
E183.8.G7W625 2005
327.41073'09'045—dc22 2005022447

ISBN: 0-7391-1164-7 (cloth : alk. paper)
ISBN: 978-0-7391-1895-5 / 0-7391-1895-1 (pbk. : alk. paper)

Printed in the United States of America

Contents

Chapter One

Britain and America in the Postwar World

Great Britain's humiliating defeat during the Suez Crisis of late 1956 clearly demonstrated that Britain's ability to act as an independent global power had come to an end. Prime Minister Anthony Eden's government discovered that it could not sustain a major overseas military operation without the support, or at least acquiescence, of the United States. The Eisenhower administration, fearful that the Anglo-French invasion of Egypt would alienate the developing world from the West, applied economic and political pressure to force the invaders to quickly withdraw. While the Suez debacle did not cause the immediate dissolution of the British Empire, it was an important turning point, as it did force London to reevaluate its policy of remaining a global power, and to accept the inevitability of reducing its overseas military and political commitments. After Suez the British government and general public had to face the fact that the days of the United Kingdom acting as a great power were over.[1]

BRITISH RESOLVE TO REMAIN A WORLD POWER

While the decline of British power after the Second World War may seem inevitable in hindsight, London made a concerted, albeit doomed, effort to remain a global power after 1945. There is no doubt that in the postwar era Britain's leaders found themselves in a difficult position. At the end of the Second World War the British Empire, the United States, and the Soviet Union shared a common victory over the Axis. Yet for Britain the triumph was bittersweet. Victory in the Second World War had cost Great Britain dearly and peace did not bring a quick return to prosperity. By 1945, as a result of the damage and expenditures of total war, Britain had lost 25 percent of its prewar national wealth. German bombing had destroyed four million homes. Industrial capacity had been reduced by wartime damage, excessive wear due to military production, and lack of investment. Before the war London had been a major world financial center and a source of capital export. By the end of the war, overseas investments had declined by 60 percent. London's gold and dollar reserves were nearly depleted. In the postwar world Britain had become a debtor nation, owing more than £3 billion to its creditors.[2]

Despite the obvious decline in British wealth as a result of the war, and the fact that empire's days were numbered, numerous historians have pointed out that for at least a decade after World War II Great Britain continued to function as a global power. John Gallagher contends that the Second World War actually sparked a short-lived revival of the empire, which had been in decline since the end of the First World War.[3] John Darwin argues that by the early 1950s Britain had, at least temporarily, stabilized its position as a "world power."[4] David Reynolds warns against the tendency to write off the British Empire after 1945, pointing out that following the United States and the Soviet Union, Great Britain "remained the world's next largest economy and military power into the 1950s."[5]

Economic and military statistics support this view of continued British power. In 1953 the United States produced 44.7 percent of the world's manufactured products, with the Soviet Union coming in a distant second with 10.7 percent. While dwarfed by the American economy, Britain still produced 8.4 percent of global output, well ahead of West Germany at 5.9 percent, France at 3.2 percent, and Japan at 2.9 percent. In terms of exported manufactured products, Britain's world share of 25.5 percent was almost equal to the 27.3 percent exported by the United States.[6] In 1953 the United Kingdom mustered over 900,000 men, a significant military force, even if not at the massive level of the Soviets with 4.75 million or the Americans with 3.5 million men. The British maintained their large military, which included more than eleven army divisions, through the method of peacetime conscription, a policy that was unprecedented in British history.[7] Britain also produced more weapons than all the other European NATO members combined and spent a greater percentage of national income on the military than the other European allies, or even the United States.[8] In addition to conventional forces, the British tested their first nuclear device in October 1952 and embarked on a hydrogen bomb program in 1954.[9] While clearly diminished in power relative to the United States and the Soviet Union, Great Britain was by no means an insignificant power and did not intend to act like one.

Under the leadership of Clement Attlee, the Labor Party provided Britain with its first postwar government. Although the Conservative Party feared that Labor would provide weak leadership, Prime Minister Attlee and his foreign secretary, Ernest Bevin, resolved to reinvigorate their nation. At home Attlee presided over the revolutionary creation of the welfare state. Abroad, his government sought to preserve as much of the British Empire as possible and maintain Britain's status as a great power.[10] This foreign policy mirrored that of Winston Churchill's wartime government, which had made defense of imperial possessions a part of Britain's global military strategy.[11]

While Britain had regained control of its entire prewar empire by 1945, a number of dramatic changes quickly occurred. Most significantly, the "Jewel in the Crown," India, received its independence in 1947. The Labor government clearly saw that the limits of Britain's power made it impossible to hold the subcontinent against the will of its inhabitants. Burma and Ceylon quickly followed suit. In 1948 London abandoned the troubled mandate of Palestine. However, Bevin intended these withdrawals to be a tactical retreat, not the first step in the dismantling of the British Empire. Even without India, Britain still had important possessions in Asia such as Singapore, Hong Kong, and Malaya. The African colonies were intact and contained untapped resources. Despite the end of the Palestinian Mandate, Britain remained the dominant imperial power in the Middle East. London hoped to sustain its global power by fostering good relations with its newly freed colonies through the expanded commonwealth and by maintaining control of the remaining parts of the empire.[12]

The emergence of the Cold War, soon after the end of the Second World War, added a new dimension to London's global strategy. Britain abandoned its long-held policy of avoiding close military ties to the continent. Fearful of the possibility of a Soviet attack, Ernest Bevin cooperated in the creation of NATO in 1949 to tie the United States to the defense of Western Europe.[13] The possibility of Communist infiltration of the colonial world also influenced British policy. Defense of the empire could now be linked to the containment of the Soviet Union. Bevin hoped that the United States, which had embraced containment as its central foreign policy goal, would prove to be a valuable ally in maintaining the British Empire as an anti-Communist bulwark. London believed that once the domestic economy revived, and the resources of the empire and commonwealth could be more fully exploited, Britain would secure her continued status as a great power.[14]

The Labor government's plan to rely on the United States to help it defend Britain's empire faced the hurdle of overcoming traditional American anti-imperialism. Washington's anticolonialism had caused tensions between the allies during the Second World War, but these problems had been somewhat ameliorated when India gained its independence. Still, the American people continued to reject the idea of colonial possessions as "un-American," and Washington worried that British imperialism might alienate popular opinion in the non-European world.[15]

The most important card that Britain had to play to deflect American anti-colonialism and receive the support from Washington that it needed was its value as a Cold War ally. Washington wanted partners to share the burden of containment, and the United Kingdom was America's chief ally. One of the reasons that Britain made the effort to remain a credible military power was to retain some influence over its more powerful American ally by demonstrating its continued strength.[16] With the French military committed to Indochina and later Algeria, and with West Germany still disarmed, the four British army divisions and supporting air force based in Germany were an essential part of the NATO command. The American B-29s that were based in the United Kingdom were an important component of Washington's nuclear strategy.[17] British military facilities from the Mediterranean to East Asia provided bases for American warships and planes. London had important contacts with local elites in Asia, Africa, and the Middle East and helped to maintain a global intelligence and signal service that could be exploited by the West.[18]

CHURCHILL RETURNS TO POWER

In October 1951, when Winston Churchill returned to 10 Downing Street, his government continued the struggle to maintain Britain's status as a global power. As had Attlee and Bevin before them, both Churchill and his foreign secretary, Anthony Eden, hoped that America would play a vital role as a British ally. Churchill, confident in his skill at personal diplomacy, believed that he would be able to influence the direction of American foreign policy to the benefit of the United Kingdom.[19] The prime minister had a sentimental attachment to the United States and firmly believed that the cultural bonds between the English-speaking peoples would cement a uniquely close political relationship. Churchill expected that the United States would be willing to seek the sage advice of London in formulating American foreign policy. He hoped to capitalize on Britain's long years as an imperial power to educate the mighty, but inexperienced, Americans in the ways of global power politics.[20]

Anthony Eden had less faith that bonds of emotion would secure Britain a "special relationship" with the United States. However, he did believe that London had to cooperate closely with Washington in order to reduce the financial and military burden of protecting the empire. Conscious of the decline of Britain's economic power, Eden planned to gradually reduce Britain's commitments to defend its global interests by creating regional security pacts with pro-British governments.[21] These new arrangements would replace the more overt imperialism of the prewar era yet protect British influence overseas. The foreign secretary saw the role of the United States as providing financial backing and additional military muscle to these regional alliances while Britain provided the political leadership. Eden reckoned that Washington would cooperate in order to facilitate the containment of the Soviet Union. If this plan worked, Britain's position as a world power would be secured in a form that appeared less "imperialistic." Eden hoped that shedding the mantle of overt imperial power would reduce the threat from African and Asian anti-colonial nationalism and placate traditional American anti-imperialism.[22]

EISENHOWER AND AMERICA AS A SUPERPOWER

Unlike Britain, America held a secure, if unfamiliar, status as a global superpower. At the close of the Second World War, American troops and bases stretched across the globe. The American navy and air force were the most powerful in the world. Until 1949, Washington enjoyed a monopoly on atomic weapons. The economic might of the United States presented an even more impressive picture than its military power. American GNP had risen during the war from $91 billion to $212 billion, raw material production increased by 60 percent, and industrial output almost tripled.[23] Great Britain, which had once used its own wealth as a tool of empire, became the recipient of vast amounts of American aid. From 1945 to 1955 the United States provided Britain with $7.67 billion in economic aid and $1 billion in military assistance.[24] The obvious inequity in economic and military power between Britain and the United States colored their relations in the postwar world.

In November 1952, a little more than a year after Churchill returned to power, the American voters elected Republican Party candidate Dwight D. Eisenhower as the next president of the United States. Eisenhower and Secretary of State John Foster Dulles inherited from Harry Truman a commitment to contain the Soviet Union and resist the spread of Communism throughout the world. Eisenhower had run an election campaign that featured tough anti-Communist rhetoric. However, once in office, Eisenhower became determined to reduce American military expenditures and end the war in Korea. The administration abandoned any hopes of quickly liberating the satellite states of the Soviet Union and launching a "rollback" of Communist power. For the foreseeable future the United States could not go onto the offensive against Communism. In order to facilitate a cut in defense spending, Washington determined to rely more heavily on nuclear weapons and the threat of "massive retaliation" as a deterrent, in lieu of more expensive conventional forces. The administration hoped that NATO would be able to bear more of the burden in Europe, particularly if West Germany could be integrated into the alliance.[25]

In addition to concern about the fiscal health of the United States, the Eisenhower administration believed that the breakup of the European colonial empires and the fate of the developing world would have an important impact on the struggle against Communist expansion. The administration believed that continued European imperialism threatened to alienate the developing world and provide an opening for Communism. Washington placed great importance on the large populations and natural resources of Asia and Africa. Tied to the West, the emerging states would be valuable allies. Alternately, Washington feared that if the Soviet Union seduced these same nations, it would add immeasurably to Communist power. However, the United States could not simply give support to every nationalist movement in the colonial world. American relations with their Western European allies, particularly the imperial powers such as Britain and France, had to be considered. Washington recognized the centrality of the NATO alliance to the containment of the Soviet Union. Moreover, in some cases, as in Malaya or Indochina, nationalism had apparently been co-opted by Communism. Under these conditions Washington supported the use of force against national liberation movements. Eisenhower's government thus found itself in a difficult position in regards to European imperialism as it tried to maintain good relations with both the colonizers and the colonized. London hoped that this American ambiguity toward colonialism could be exploited to save the British Empire.

ANGLO-AMERICAN RELATIONS AND THE CONTINUATION OF BRITISH POWER

The aim of this book is to examine Anglo-American relations in the last years before the Suez Crisis to judge how successful Great Britain was in retaining its position as an independent world power. While tied together by a mutual fear of Soviet expansionism, it is clear that London and Washington were bound to come into conflict in the 1950s. The principal goal of Britain's foreign policy was to stop the erosion of its power. America's overwhelming concern was to stop the expansion of Communism. At times these aims came into conflict. The central question addressed by this work is how these conflicts were resolved by the allies. Did Great Britain possess the strength to pursue policies that were at odds with those of the United States? Was Britain successful in exploiting its importance as a Cold War ally to influence American foreign policy? Did the American alliance help the British to maintain their position as a global power?

This work consists of four case studies that examine different diplomatic controversies that shed light on the state of Anglo-American relations from

1953 to 1955. The four cases under examination include the debate surrounding Churchill's drive to convene an East-West Summit, Anglo-American negotiations concerning the supply of arms to Iraq, the Anglo-Saudi dispute over the Buraimi Oasis, and the so-called First Offshore Islands Crisis involving the United States and the People's Republic of China. The use of case studies enables this work to explore several diplomatic incidents in depth, while also providing a wide scope by focusing on different geographical areas. The cases chosen illustrate a number of different types of disagreements in Anglo-American relations from overarching issues of East-West détente, to competition for influence in a single Middle Eastern nation.

The summit issue revolved around Churchill's plan to settle the major issues of the Cold War in Europe through direct negotiations between the Western leaders and Soviet Premier Georgy Malenkov. Churchill had great faith in direct talks as a means to reduce the international tensions caused by the Cold War. He believed that the West had to coexist with the Soviet Union or risk the catastrophe of a nuclear war. The Eisenhower administration, and indeed most of the British Cabinet, disapproved of Churchill's scheme and attempted to dissuade the prime minister from supporting a summit conference. This case stands as an example of a disagreement on the fundamental issue of East-West relations and involved the highest officials and leaders of both nations. Specifically it focused on the value of détente versus confrontation. These issues would define the purpose of the Western alliance. This chapter will attempt to answer several questions. How far would Churchill be willing to push the reluctant Americans toward adopting his goal of détente? Was Churchill ready to pursue closer relations with Moscow even without American support? What pressures did Washington bring to bear on the aging prime minister to attempt to get him to abandon his plans?

The next two case studies illuminate different aspects of Anglo-American relations in the explosive Middle East. One major point of contention arose from London's fear the United States intended to replace British power in the Middle East with an informal American empire. At times in the early 1950s Anglo-American competition for influence in the region was heated. The disagreement over Iraq is a good example of how this competition played out in negotiations between the Foreign Office and the State Department over supplying aid to a single country. In Iraq, long a client state of the British, London and Washington faced the question of whether or not the Iraqis should be supplied with a grant of military aid from the United States. The British suspected that Washington intended to displace them as Baghdad's chief ally by becoming the principal arms supplier for the Iraqi military. This incident raises some interesting questions. How successful was London in protecting its position in Iraq from American competition? Did

Washington really plan to displace the British in Iraq? Was Eden's plan of inviting limited American involvement in the Middle East in order to reduce Britain's expenditures, while maintaining London's political clout in the region, a viable strategy?

The second Middle Eastern case study deals with the competing claims to the Buraimi Oasis by Saudi Arabia and the British-allied Trucial States. This case shows us an example of how a direct challenge to British imperial interests could cause a serious disagreement between London and Washington by highlighting the clash between the American Cold War agenda and Britain's imperial aims. The British saw defending the interests of its allies at Buraimi as a vital test of its prestige in the Middle East. Washington, on the other hand, hoped to avoid alienating Riyadh. The Saudis were the closest Arab allies of the United States and were seen by Washington as a valuable asset in the drive to contain Communism. After Saudi forces seized the oasis, the United Kingdom had agreed, under a plan facilitated by the United States, to refrain from the immediate use of force and attempt a peaceful settlement to the dispute. In the meantime the Saudis lobbied Washington for political support in favor of their claim while the British prepared to use military force to achieve their aims if the Saudis proved inflexible. This chapter raises the question of how much power Britain was able to employ in the Middle East without American approval in the years before Suez.

The final case study moves to East Asia and returns to the broader issues of Western relations with Communism that were seen in the summit chapter. However, in this case the focus is on Communist China and involves the immediate threat of nuclear war. The First Offshore Island Crisis broke out in 1954 when the People's Liberation Army began to shell the Nationalist occupied islands just off the Chinese mainland. The United States felt compelled to support Chiang Kai-shek's hold over these small islands. In this highly charged atmosphere the British and Americans disagreed on the best course of action. An examination of Anglo-American relations during the crisis will reveal the level of success that Washington achieved in its bid to secure the cooperation of its ally in what the Americans saw as a crucial test of will with Communist China as well as the impact that Britain had on the formulation of American policy. The chapter will also provide some insight into the wider issue of Anglo-American disagreements on the best way to confront Communist expansion in Asia.

Taken as a whole these case studies should provide some important insights into the level of independence that Great Britain was able to exercise in foreign affairs prior to 1956 and therefore the extent to which Britain remained a global power in its own right and avoided relegation to the status of America's Cold War client.

NOTES

1. Anne Orde, *The Eclipse of Great Britain: The United States and Imperial Decline, 1895–1956* (New York, 1996), 192; David Reynolds, *Britannia Overruled: British Policy and World Power in the Twentieth Century* (New York, 2000), 193.

2. John Darwin, *Britain and Decolonization: The Retreat from Empire in the Post-War World* (New York, 1988), 65–68, 131; Robert Hathaway, *Great Britain and the United States: Special Relations Since World War II* (Boston, 1990), 10.

3. John Gallagher, *The Decline, Revival, and Fall of the British Empire* (New York, 1982), 73.

4. Darwin, *Britain and Decolonization*, 166.

5. David Reynolds, "Rethinking Anglo-American Relations," *International Affairs* 65, no. 1 (Winter 1988/89): 108.

6. Reynolds, *Britannia Overruled*, 10–11.

7. Michael Dockrill, *British Defense Since 1945* (New York, 1988), 36–37, 51.

8. Reynolds, *Britannia Overruled*, 21, 163; Malcolm Chalmers, *Paying for Defense: Military Spending and British Decline* (London, 1985), 46.

9. Reynolds, *Britannia Overruled*, 171.

10. Gallagher, *The Decline, Revival, and Fall*, 141–53.

11. David Reynolds, "Roosevelt, Churchill, and the Wartime Anglo-American Alliance," in *The 'Special Relationship': Anglo-American Relations Since 1945*, edited by Wm. Roger Louis and Headly Bull (Oxford, 1986), 20–27.

12. Darwin, *Britain and Decolonization*, 122–25.

13. Hathaway, *Great Britain and the United States*, 25.

14. C. J. Bartlett, *"The Special Relationship": A Political History of Anglo-American Relations Since 1945* (New York, 1992), 15–16.

15. Orde, *The Eclipse of Great Britain*, 5; Wm. Roger Louis, "American Anti-Colonialism and the Dissolution of the British Empire," in *The 'Special Relationship': Anglo-American Relations Since 1945*, edited by Wm. Roger Louis and Headly Bull (Oxford, 1986), 267–68; Hathaway, *Great Britain and the United States*, 22.

16. Malcolm Chalmers, *Paying for Defense: Military Spending and British Decline* (London, 1985), 47.

17. David Reynolds, "A 'Special Relationship'? America, Britain and the International Order Since the Second World War," *International Affairs* 62, no. 1 (Winter 1985/1986): 8.

18. David Dimbleby and David Reynolds, *An Ocean Apart: The Relationship Between Britain and America in the Twentieth Century* (New York, 1988), 212.

19. Peter Boyle, "The 'Special Relationship' with Washington," in *The Foreign Policy of Churchill's Peacetime Administration, 1951–55*, edited by John Young (Worcester, UK, 1988), 29–31.

20. Sir Michael Howard, "Afterward: 'The Special Relationship,'" in *The 'Special Relationship': Anglo-American Relations Since 1945*, edited by Wm. Roger Louis and Bull Headly (Oxford, 1986), 411.

21. Anthony Adamthwaite, "Introduction: The Foreign Office and Policy-making," in *The Foreign Policy of Churchill's Peacetime Administration, 1951–1955*, edited by

John Young (Worchester, UK, 1988), 9; Evelyn Shuckburgh, *Descent to Suez: Diaries, 1951–56* (New York, 1986), 210.

22. Hathaway, *Great Britain and the United States*, 10.

23. Hathaway, *Great Britain and the United States*, 36–38.

24. Bartlett, "*The Special Relationship*," 61–62; Chester J. Pach Jr. and Elmo Richardson, *The Presidency of Dwight D. Eisenhower* (Lawrence, KS, 1991), 75–82.

25. Robert Bowie and Richard Immerman, *Waging Peace: How Eisenhower Shaped an Enduring Cold War Strategy* (New York, 1998), 213–14.

Chapter Two

Debate over Détente: Churchill's Summit Proposal

During his peacetime premiership Winston Churchill obsessively pursued a summit meeting between Great Britain, the United States, and the Soviet Union aimed at reducing the tensions of the Cold War. According to the major works on the subject, Churchill's move toward détente arose from a number of factors. John Young argues that Churchill wanted to leave a legacy not only as a great leader during war but also as a man of peace. Churchill believed that as long as the West remained united and strong in the face of Soviet power, an agreement that recognized a Soviet sphere of influence in Eastern Europe would be an acceptable price to pay for peace. In fact, Churchill thought that the terrible destructive power of thermonuclear weapons made peace the only option if Britain was to survive at all. The prime minster believed that eventually Communism would collapse because it denied the basic human need for freedom and desire for economic well-being. Therefore, it was his conviction that the world need only avoid nuclear war, and in the long run the Soviet Union would collapse due to internal decay. In *Churchill's Cold War: The Politics of Personal Diplomacy*, Klaus Larres proposes additional motivations to those advanced by Young. Larres believes that Churchill had always had a deep faith in the efficacy of personal diplomacy, and that his summit plan was only the last example of this tendency. Moreover, Churchill understood that if Great Britain hoped to remain a world power in its own right, and not simply an American auxiliary, the Cold War would have to be de-escalated so that Britain could focus its energy on developing its economic strength, not on the containment of the Soviet Union. Thus, in the early 1950s, Churchill, the great anti-Communist, became a determined advocate for détente.[1]

The Eisenhower administration exhibited much less enthusiasm for détente and summitry with the Soviets. The Republican White House needed to be careful not to offend the fiercely anti-Communist wing of its own party, to whom any agreement with Moscow could likely be deemed a sellout. However, the administration's reticence to pursue détente was not solely produced by fear of the McCarthyites. Eisenhower and Dulles were much more suspicious of the Kremlin than were the British, and Washington doubted that the Soviets would sincerely engage in peace talks. The United States believed that the first order of business in Europe should be solidifying NATO and integrating a rearmed Germany into the alliance.[2] Of course the British did not reject these goals, but London approached the Soviet question from a less single-minded view. Here we must ask what this difference of opinion on détente reveals about the nature of the relationship between London and Washington and whether or not it demonstrates a continued role for Great Britain as a world power.

EISENHOWER TAKES THE HELM

Churchill was extremely anxious to meet Eisenhower after the latter's election in November 1952. In December, Churchill suggested that the two leaders meet informally in New York City during Churchill's New Year's visit to his old friend Bernard Baruch.[3] At their first meeting, Churchill told Eisenhower that he hoped to reestablish with the newly elected president the same close, informal relationship that he had enjoyed with Roosevelt. Eisenhower replied that he also looked forward to a very close relationship with the prime minister, but stressed that decisions of state must be made through regular channels.[4] The president-elect's words indicated that he meant to be cautious when dealing with Churchill and did not want to encourage any idea that the two men would be plotting the course of the Western Alliance by themselves. Eisenhower did not indicate that he planned to treat Britain with more respect that America's other Western European allies.

Eisenhower was first to raise the topic of a summit meeting with the Soviets. Eisenhower mentioned the possibility of using his inaugural address to offer to meet Stalin alone, at any location, and asked for Churchill's opinion. The prime minister cautiously replied that given the fact that American power clearly eclipsed that of Britain, he could raise no objection to the president meeting Stalin without him. However, Churchill advised Eisenhower to wait before making such an offer. The prime minister suggested that a Soviet-American summit that failed to produce any results would be a grave disappointment to a world hungry for peace. Despite Churchill's cautious tone Eisenhower remained open to the idea of East-West contact. He told Churchill that he had no objections to the prime minister meeting Stalin man-to-man if he thought it would do any good.[5]

This interchange is intriguing, especially given Churchill's subsequent obsession with a summit meeting and Eisenhower's resistance to the idea. The president must have caught Churchill off-guard with his bold proposal to meet Stalin. Instead of arguing that a three-power summit would be preferable, the prime minister urged Eisenhower to go slow on negotiations with the Soviets. At the time, future American Ambassador to Moscow Charles Bohlen questioned Churchill's motivation. Bohlen asked a British Embassy official if Churchill's coolness toward an Eisenhower-Stalin meeting resulted from a fear that he would be left out, or whether the prime minister had genuinely changed his mind on the value of an early East-West summit.[6] In the view of Anthony Eden and other Foreign Office officials, Churchill spoke from fear that Stalin would take advantage of Eisenhower's naïveté, therefore the prime minister wished to proceed slowly toward a meeting.[7] However, Churchill's later determination to pursue a summit, despite numerous obstacles, suggests that Churchill's chief objection to an Eisenhower-Stalin meeting was that he would not be involved. Aside from the desire to have a role on the world stage Churchill may also have believed that only he had the skills of personal diplomacy to make an East-West summit successful.[8] In January 1953 the Foreign Office, which subsequently urged restraint on the summit idea, may have been engaged in wishful thinking in suggesting that Churchill wanted to take a wait-and-see attitude toward the Soviet Union.

In any case, this first instance in which the summit question arose did not cause any strain in Anglo-American relations. The possibility of a high-level meeting had not been seriously discussed in New York, and Churchill certainly did not press the idea on Eisenhower. It seems likely, however, that Churchill came away from the discussions with his old wartime colleague with the opinion that Eisenhower favored the idea of a summit and that Churchill would be able to arrange a three-power meeting when he judged the time was right. Churchill clearly believed that Britain would be able to provide valuable guidance to its more powerful ally when it came to East-West relations.

THE DEATH OF STALIN

On March 5, 1953, Joseph Stalin died and a collective leadership replaced the Soviet dictator. The nominal head of the Soviet government and Communist Party, Georgi Malenkov, shared power with Lavrenti Beria, who controlled the Interior and Security Ministries, and Vyacheslav Molotov, who was reappointed as foreign minister. This new Soviet triumvirate quickly began to make overtures of peace toward the West. At Stalin's funeral Malenkov raised the possibility of détente. On March 15, 1953, he announced to the Supreme Soviet that all existing international disputes could and should "be decided by peaceful means, on the basis of mutual understanding." The motivation for this so-called "peace offensive" by the Soviet Union is still in dispute. A genuine fear of war with the United States may have played a role in Moscow's thinking on détente. Recent evidence suggests that Malenkov and Beria hoped to ease East-West tensions in order to concentrate on consolidating Communism in Russia and the Eastern bloc. It is equally possible that Molotov hoped to divide the West by offering to negotiate. In the spring of 1953 the Western Alliance continued to struggle with the dilemma of how to integrate West Germany into its military structure. The proposed European Defense Community (EDC) had not yet cleared the hurdle of ratification by the French Assembly. EDC called for the continental European states of the Western Alliance to form a joint military formation, in effect a Western European army. While most states would retain a separate national military, a rearmed West Germany would have all of its units in the new EDC army. French critics of EDC, who opposed rearming Germany under any circumstances, would have been tempted to make a deal with the Soviets if it could mean that Germany would not be rearmed. Even if EDC was not killed outright by peace negotiations, Molotov may have hoped to seriously delay the ratification.[9]

Churchill's interest in détente received a boost from Stalin's death. According to his personal physician Lord Moran, Churchill saw the change in Soviet leadership as "an opportunity that will not recur" to relax East-West tensions. Moran recorded that Churchill seemed "to think of little else."[10] On the other hand, Anthony Eden and the Foreign Office did not share Churchill's belief that Stalin's death created an opportunity to settle important issues with the Soviets. The Foreign Office interpreted the Soviet "peace offensive" as a ploy designed to derail EDC. The prime minister's enthusiasm continued unabated despite the views of his diplomatic advisers.[11]

On March 10, 1953, Churchill sent a message questioning Eisenhower about his view of a summit with the Soviets:

> I am sure that everyone will want to know whether you still contemplate a meeting with the Soviets. I remember our talk [in January 1953] when you told me I was welcome to meet Stalin if I thought fit and that you intended to offer to do so. I understood this as meaning that you did not want us to go together, but now that there is no more Stalin I wonder whether this makes any difference to your view about separate approaches. . . . I have the feeling that we might, both of us, together or separately, be called to account if no attempt were made to turn over a leaf so that a new page would be started with something more coherent on it than a series of casual and dangerous incidents at the many points of contact between the two divisions of the world.[12]

In this cable Churchill dropped his earlier advice for Eisenhower to proceed cautiously on negotiations with Moscow and suggested that a three-power summit might now be in order.

In Washington the administration almost universally saw the "peace offensive" as an attempt to disrupt Western unity and promote neutralism among the European nations. While some disagreement existed within the government as to how the United States should respond, Eisenhower decided that he would make a public statement, cautiously treating the Soviet peace feelers as genuine.[13]

On March 12, 1953, Eisenhower responded to Churchill's query. The president began by assuring Churchill that "the subject raised in your message . . . has been engaging our attention here for some days. We are convinced that a move giving to the world some promise of hope, which will have the virtues of simplicity and persuasiveness, should be made quickly." However, Eisenhower went on to argue against a summit meeting. He informed Churchill that "even now I tend to doubt the wisdom of a formal multilateral meeting since this would give our opponents the same kind of opportunity they have so often had to use such meetings simultaneously to balk every reasonable effort of ourselves and to make the whole occurrence another propaganda mill." He went on to suggest that instead of an East-West summit the next step for the West should be for the United States, Britain, and "probably France" to "agree upon some general purpose and program under which each would have a specific part to play."[14] Eisenhower's letter shows that Washington was more concerned with promoting Western unity than in making a rapid diplomatic overture to Moscow in the wake of Stalin's death.

Churchill took some time in replying to Eisenhower, not sending a cable in response until April 5, 1953. "I am sure that we shall be in agreement with you that we must remain vigilantly on our guard and maintain all the process of defensive rearmament from which any real improvement must have resulted," he wrote.

> We think, as I am sure that you do also, that we ought to lose no chance of finding out how far the Malenkov regime are prepared to go in easing things up all around. . . . It may be that presently the Soviets will make overtures for some form of direct discussion of world problems whether on a Four Power basis or in some other manner. I assume of course that we shall deal in the closest collaboration with any such overtures if they are made.[15]

In this message Churchill tried to reassure the president that he had not weakened in his resolve to resist Communism. However, he continued to urge Eisenhower to keep open the possibilities of meeting the Soviets and stressed the importance of Anglo-American cooperation on the whole issue of negotiation with

Moscow. The death of Stalin seemed to push Churchill to make a bid for détente sooner rather than later, but the Eisenhower administration exhibited greater skepticism toward Soviet policy.

THE "CHANCE FOR PEACE" SPEECH

In spite of its cautious attitude toward a summit, the Eisenhower administration did plan to make a public gesture on the issue of peace. On April 9, 1953, Eisenhower sent a letter to Churchill expressing his intention of delivering a speech on the issue of East-West relations, together with a draft of the proposed address. The president expressed his hope that a formal speech would "delineate . . . the specific steps or measures that we believe necessary" to improve relations with the Soviet Union. Eisenhower reassured Churchill that the United States would never move forward on détente without the agreement of Great Britain.[16] In the draft of the speech shown to Churchill, Eisenhower called on the Soviets to provide proof of their good intentions by signing an armistice in Korea, as well as making provisions to end the occupation of Austria and the division of Germany.[17]

At the time that Eisenhower's draft arrived in London, Eden was about to go into the hospital for a gallstones operation and Churchill had begun to act as his own foreign secretary. As of yet, no one knew that Eden's health problems would keep him from his duties for nearly six months. Just days before Eden's first operation he had agreed with Churchill's assessment that the president's speech might be too anti-Soviet in tone. Accordingly, the prime minister dispatched a cable to Eisenhower urging him to take a wait-and-see attitude on negotiations. Churchill told the president, "I believe myself that at this moment time is on our side. The apparent change of Soviet mood is so new and so indefinite and the causes for it so obscure that there could not be much risk in letting things develop." The prime minister urged Eisenhower to focus on the task of achieving an armistice in Korea and to remove from his speech the specific American terms for an agreement lest this only delay settlement. He concluded by stating,

> Anthony [Eden] and I . . . hope that our arguments will persuade you to bide your time. We cannot see what you would lose by waiting till the full character and purpose of the Soviet change is more clearly defined and also is apparent to the whole free world. I always like the story of Napoleon going to sleep . . . as the battle began saying, "Wake me when their infantry column gets beyond the wood."[18]

On April 12, 1953, Eisenhower informed Churchill that he would modify the part of his speech concerning the Korean armistice. However, as far as delaying the address, Eisenhower wrote that "of course no one can accurately gauge the probable influence of an early statement as opposed to a later one," but he remained determined to deliver a speech on the general issue of East-West relations.[19] Churchill quickly cabled back, saying, "You may be sure that we shall stand by you on fundamentals. The question of timing did, however, press upon me. It would be a pity if a sudden frost nipped spring in the bud." The prime minister went on to urge Eisenhower "to combine the re-assertions of your and our inflexible resolves with some balancing expression of hope that we have entered upon a new era."[20] Two days later, Eisenhower wrote to Churchill assuring him, "I agree with the tenor of your comments and shall certainly strive to make my talk one that will not freeze the tender buds of sprouting decency, if indeed they are really coming out."[21]

On April 16, 1953, Eisenhower delivered his planned address to the Society of Newspaper Editors. It became known as the "Chance for Peace" speech. Despite Churchill's subtle urging not to offend the Soviet leaders with a harsh speech, the president's address placed the blame for the deterioration of peace after 1945 squarely on the Soviets, claiming that Moscow had sought to guarantee its own security at the expense of others. Eisenhower went on to denounce the heavy cost of defending against Soviet aggression. The arms race, he said, constituted "a theft from those who hunger and are not fed, those who are cold and are not clothed. This world in arms is not spending money alone. It is spending the sweat of its laborers, the genius of its scientists, the hopes of its children." Before any negotiations, Eisenhower demanded concrete proof from Moscow that it wanted peace, such as an armistice in Korea, an end to the war in Indochina, and free elections to reunite Germany.[22]

Secretary of State John Foster Dulles followed up the "Chance for Peace" speech with his own address to the same group only two days later. Dulles stressed containment and deterrence. He said the West had to keep its guard up and should increase aid to the French in Indochina. According to one study of the administration's Cold War policy, Eisenhower saw nothing inconsistent in these two speeches. The president believed that peace depended not on any concession from the West but on a fundamental change in Soviet policy. In the president's mind the next move had to come from the Soviets. However, the speech had not been well received in Moscow.[23]

Once Eisenhower delivered his speech Churchill dropped his talk of caution and sought to persuade Washington to pursue détente more actively. Although events had not developed as he had hoped, Churchill must have believed that it was now time for him to weigh in with his own proposal for a summit meeting. On April 17, 1953, in a speech in Glasgow, Churchill spoke about the possibility that Stalin's death might have created a positive "change of mood" in the Soviet Union. Churchill's Cabinet held a considerably more skeptical opinion of the Soviet "peace offensive," believing that it would be very dangerous for the West to be lulled into any false sense of security by Moscow.[24] Despite the concerns of his ministers, Churchill made his first outright proposal for a three-power summit in a letter to Eisenhower on April 21, 1953. He complimented the president's speech and pointedly questioned him about "the next step." Churchill stated,

> There will . . . be a strong movement here for a meeting between Heads of State and Governments. How do you stand on this? In my opinion the best would be that the three victorious Powers, who separated at Potsdam in 1945, should come together again. . . . If nothing can be arranged I shall have to consider seriously a personal contact. You told me in New York [in January 1953] you would have no objection to this.[25]

The president tried to dissuade Churchill from seeking a summit. Eisenhower wrote,

> As to the next step, I feel that we should not rush things too much and should await the Soviet reply or reaction longer than a few days. There is some feeling here also [for a Summit meeting] but I do not think this should be allowed to press us into precipitate initiatives. . . . We have so far seen no concrete Soviet actions, which would indicate their willingness to perform in connection with the larger issues. In the circumstances we would risk raising hopes of progress toward an accommodation that would not be justified. This is not to say, of course, that I do not envisage the possible desirability at an appropriate time that the three Western Powers and the Soviets come together.

The president went on to say that as the situation had changed since they spoke in January, it would be better if Churchill did not make an independent approach to Moscow. If Churchill felt that he had to seek "a personal contact," Eisenhower asked for "as much advance notice as you could possibly give us."[26]

The British prime minister would not be as easily put off on his idea of a summit meeting as Eisenhower may have hoped. While he did not press his argument with Washington at this time, on April 28 Churchill mentioned in the Cabinet that he still hoped to finish the business left undone at Potsdam. He pointed out to his colleagues a newspaper quote by Molotov that Moscow remained willing to discuss any issue with the West.[27]

The interchange between Churchill and Eisenhower during the period of the "Chance for Peace" speech saw the firming-up of their opinions on the wisdom of an early summit meeting. Churchill originally advised Eisenhower to take his time in negotiating with the Soviets and to concentrate on ending the

Korean War. The reasons for Churchill's caution are not entirely clear. As suggested above, he and Eden believed that Eisenhower's speech was not sufficiently conciliatory. Other factors probably played a role. Perhaps Churchill feared, as he had at the time of the president's inauguration, that Eisenhower might issue a call for a Soviet-American summit that would exclude the British. It is possible that he felt constrained by the skeptical view of his own Foreign Office on the Soviet "peace offensive." However, once Eisenhower delivered his speech, the prime minister quickly called for a diplomatic follow-up to maintain momentum. From that point on, Churchill would be a nearly constant advocate for a three-power summit while the Eisenhower administration, and indeed his own Cabinet, sought to restrain him. A pattern also emerged by April 1953 in which Eisenhower tactfully tried to get Churchill to abandon the summit idea, while the prime minister refused to accept this judgment and tried to convert Washington to his point of view.

CHURCHILL'S PUBLIC CALL FOR A SUMMIT

In May 1953 Churchill began to discuss pursuing his dream of a summit with or without approval by the United States. Foreign Office officials attempted to dissuade the prime minister. In a conversation on May 3, 1953, Deputy Under Secretary of State for Foreign Affairs Sir Pierson Dixon warned Churchill that the Foreign Office had serious reservations about any Anglo-Soviet talks. Dixon believed that Moscow would attempt to drive a wedge between the United States and Britain and weaken French resolve to support EDC. Churchill remained convinced that the possible benefits of establishing good relations with the Soviet leadership outweighed the risks.[28] The prime minister sent a cable to Eisenhower on the same day proposing that he and Eden visit Moscow to meet with Malenkov and Molotov for informal talks.[29] Churchill explained to his skeptical Foreign Office colleagues that if Eisenhower disapproved of a British visit to Moscow, he would probably not go, but he would try to draw the president into articulating an alternative policy. Churchill said that even if the United States would do nothing to further negotiations with Moscow, he believed that he had to make some attempt to break the deadlock of the Cold War himself. Permanent Under Secretary of State for Foreign Affairs Sir William Strang speculated that Churchill "conceives that a special charge is laid upon him to use his unrivaled position and influence for the good of mankind."[30] Whatever Churchill's view of his own destiny, it seems clear that he sought to force Eisenhower's hand. If the prime minister could begin movement toward détente, he hoped that he might induce Washington into following his lead.

On May 5, 1953, Eisenhower sent a fairly strongly worded reply to Churchill declaring that he and Dulles advised against a trip to Moscow. He went on to write,

> You will pardon me I know, if I express a bit of astonishment that you think it appropriate to recommend Moscow to Molotov as a suitable meeting place. . . . In my note to you of April 25 I expressed the view that we should not rush things too much and should not permit feelings in our countries for a meeting between heads of states and governments to press us into precipitous initiatives. I feel just as strongly now as I did ten days ago that this is right.

Eisenhower added that he doubted Moscow's sincerity, as the Communists had not become less aggressive in Asia. Like the Foreign Office, Eisenhower warned Churchill that an Anglo-Soviet summit would only serve to upset the French and other NATO members. Finally, the president hinted that Congress would be so upset that it might not renew a reciprocal trade agreement with Britain.[31] Significantly, this veiled threat of economic retaliation never materialized and was never repeated.

Churchill continued to argue his point in a follow-up cable to Eisenhower. The prime minister argued that much goodwill could be obtained from the Soviets by visiting Moscow. He pointed to his October 1944 trip to see Stalin, which resulted in the "Percentages Deal," as an example of what could be gained from direct negotiations. "I am not afraid of the 'solitary pilgrimage' if I am sure in my heart that it may help forward the cause of peace and, even at worst, can only do harm to my reputation," he wrote. "I have a strong hope that Soviet self-interest will be their guide . . . [and] bring about an easier state of affairs." Churchill contended that as he was "only a head of government and not of state," it would be acceptable for him to visit Moscow. The most telling part of the cable came at the end where Churchill revealed his hope for a three-power summit. "Of course I would rather go with you to any place you might appoint, and that I believe is the best chance of a good result," Churchill wrote. He then promised Eisenhower that due to the need to consult the Cabinet, and because of the upcoming coronation of Elizabeth II, he would, at any rate, not go before the end of June. The prime minister closed by suggesting that by that time Eisenhower might "feel able to propose some combined action."[32]

Eisenhower's reply again stressed the opposition of the United States government to a summit meeting under the prevailing political conditions. The president suggested that rather than seeking an overall solution to the problems of East-West relations, the Western Alliance should concentrate on specific trouble spots in Asia and continue to build up their collective defense. However, Eisenhower left the door to détente slightly ajar by telling Churchill that "whenever you have an idea—even a piece of one—that might suggest a possibility of us diminishing the burdens that we are compelled to lay upon our collective peoples, please let me know about it. I should certainly ponder it. I hope my comments do not offend—I assure you I welcome yours."[33]

The possibility that Eisenhower could have offended Churchill seems very remote. The prime minister exhibited a very single-minded determination to achieve a summit, and a hardy conviction of the validity of his plan. Churchill now rejected his own earlier advice to proceed slowly. The prime minister was on the verge of publicly committing to the idea of a summit meeting. In the exchange between the two leaders in the first days of May it appears that Churchill attempted to coerce the president into calling for a three-power summit to avoid a "solitary pilgrimage" by the prime minister. It seems likely that Churchill reckoned that the Americans would be so anxious to avoid a division in the Western ranks, which an Anglo-Soviet summit might cause, that they would agree to participate in a three-power meeting.

Despite the lack of support from Washington, Churchill made a formal proposal for a summit on May 11, 1953, when he made an appeal for détente in a speech in the House of Commons. Instead of pursuing his goal with behind-the-scenes diplomacy, he openly declared to the world his support for a high-level meeting. In his speech Churchill admitted that it would prove unlikely that a complete settlement of the Cold War could be achieved. However, he said that "piecemeal solutions of individual problems should not be disdained or improvidently put aside." The prime minister offered a concrete suggestion to settle the problem of the Soviet Union's legitimate security concerns. An eastern version of the 1925 Locarno Treaty that guaranteed the Franco-German border could be created to maintain peace between the Soviet Union and Germany. Churchill envisioned Poland acting as "a buffer, though not I trust, a puppet State." To facilitate the easing of tensions Churchill proposed a summit meeting "confined to the smallest number of Powers and persons possible." The conference, he said, should be informal and "should not be overhung by a ponderous or rigid agenda, or led into mazes and jungles of technical details, zealously contested by hordes of experts and officials drawn up in vast, cumbrous array." The speech had been given without prior consultation of the Cabinet and caused an ailing Anthony Eden to remark, "It must be long in history since any one speech did so much damage to its own side."[34] Despite the fact that the Foreign Office had advised against a summit out of fear for Western unity, the speech proved very popular with both parties in Parliament.[35] Gallup polls showed that 77 percent of the British public, and even more of the American public, favored a summit meeting. The sheer popularity of the idea made it difficult for its opponents in the British government to criticize the proposal.[36]

In a press conference on May 14, 1953, Eisenhower did his best to distance the United States from Churchill's proposed summit. The president told the assembled journalists that Churchill's speech arose from "the free world's great longing for some kind of peaceful composition of our difficulties in the world, and all of us share them." However, Eisenhower went on to say that before any summit, he wanted more proof that the Soviets would negotiate in "good faith." The president also said that while summitry had a role to play in negotiations, he would prefer to begin at the level of foreign ministers to tackle the complicated problems of East-West relations.[37]

Behind the scenes, there was more concern about the impact of the May 11 address on Anglo-American relations. American Ambassador to Britain Winthrop Aldrich expressed his opinion of the speech in a letter to the State Department. Aldrich cogently argued that Churchill's motivation sprang from three sources: a genuine desire for peace, sensitivity to charges that he was a warmonger, and a desire to place a capstone on his career with one last dramatic success. Aldrich expressed concern that public pressure in Britain would force Churchill to pursue his plan with or without the support of the United States. The ambassador pointed out that

> for the first time in a major address on foreign affairs, Churchill did not mention [the] Anglo-American alliance or the necessity [of] solidarity with [the] United States. . . . While his speech was characteristic of the Churchillian temperament, it also reflects serious British misgivings about the present state of Anglo-American relations."[38]

Aldrich's fear of an Anglo-American breach over the summit issue was exaggerated. Churchill clearly intended his speech to put pressure on the United States to agree to a summit by placing public support behind the idea. Churchill remained convinced that a three-power summit held the key to peace. The prime minister had no intention of causing a rift in Anglo-American relations; in fact, he still hoped to convince the unwilling Eisenhower to participate in a summit.

Soon after the May 11 speech, French officials suggested that the three Western powers hold a summit before making any overtures to the Soviet Union. Eisenhower took the lead in scheduling a meeting to be held in Bermuda in July 1953. The three principal participants had different agendas for the conference. Churchill saw the meeting as an opportunity to prepare for a coming summit with the Soviet Union. French Premier Joseph Laniel wanted to ensure that France would not be left out of the decision-making process on the formation of a Western position on Germany. Eisenhower hoped that the French would assist the United States in talking Churchill out of a summit meeting with Moscow.[39] However, the proposed meeting was canceled because Churchill could not attend.

On June 23, 1953, the prime minister suffered a massive stroke. As fate would have it, on that same day Eden underwent a major operation in the United States to repair the botched operation he had had in April. While Churchill made a remarkable recovery, it is likely that he would have been forced to resign if Eden had been healthy or Parliament had been in session.[40] Even while stricken, a melancholy Churchill ruminated about a summit. He confided to Lord Moran on June 25, 1953, "I have stretched out a hand to grasp the paw of the Russian bear. Great things seemed within my grasp. Not perhaps world peace, but world easement. I feel I could have changed the bias of the world. America is very powerful but very clumsy. . . . I could have made her more sensible."[41] The stroke may have only increased Churchill's determination to pursue a high-level meeting. Arteriosclerosis, a hardening of the arteries that causes strokes, tends to create mental inflexibility in its sufferers. The disease also tends to magnify existing personality traits, thus it may have made Churchill even more stubborn and willful than normal.[42] In any case, a summit, with American participation, remained uppermost in his mind.

WASHINGTON FOREIGN MINISTERS CONFERENCE

In lieu of the canceled Bermuda meeting, the Western powers agreed to hold a foreign ministers conference in Washington in July 1953. This conference touched on a number of issues of mutual importance to the allies, including Churchill's proposed summit. In early July Churchill wrote to Eisenhower reaffirming his faith in a top-level meeting. He concluded that, while Western resolve needed to be maintained, the change in Soviet behavior could not be attributed simply to fear of the West. The West needed to take a risk that Moscow really was ready to negotiate a reduction in tensions. The prime minister wrote that "it is this feeling that makes me so anxious that before we reject all hope of a Soviet change of heart we should convince our peoples" that the Western governments had done everything possible to secure peace.[43]

The acting foreign secretary, Lord Salisbury, informed the Cabinet that in order to satisfy public expectation of a summit he would, "without pressing the Americans too hard at the moment, at least clear the way for a possible high-level meeting with the Soviet leaders." Salisbury also intended to reaffirm the policy of integrating West Germany into the Western alliance, give continued support to Adenauer, press for the ratification of EDC, and discourage Dulles "from any dangerous new initiatives intended to provoke early liberation movements behind the Iron Curtain."[44] Salisbury's agenda, of which the summit constituted only a small part, reflected the widely held view in the British government that Western unity outweighed the need to seek top-level talks with Moscow.

The State Department prepared for the Washington conference by reaffirming its opposition to a summit in an internal memo. However, the document recommended that the United States avoid taking the blame as the one nation responsible for blocking the summit. In order to accomplish this, the United States might propose a four-power foreign ministers conference, which Eisenhower would only attend if concrete agreement had been reached on an issue such as an Austrian treaty.[45]

At the first tripartite meeting on July 10, 1953, Salisbury dutifully raised the issue of an East-West summit. Instead of pressing for an early meeting at the top, however, the acting foreign secretary called on the allies to reaffirm "the plan for holding four-power talks with Russia at a suitable time. This was desirable in itself and also to satisfy public opinion." He agreed with Dulles that a "suitable time" would not arise until France ratified EDC. French Foreign Minister Georges Bidault countered that the French legislature would only ratify EDC after it became convinced that the German question could not be settled by negotiation with Moscow.[46]

On the following day Salisbury presented the case for a summit in a rather more cautious, but persuasive, tone. He stated, "None of us were convinced that the changes in the USSR represented a change of heart. They were rather a modification of tactics, and in the British view the object of four-power talks should be to find out more about the significance of this modification. Basic Soviet aims were still to prevent rearmament in the West and, above all, the integration of Germany with the Western defense community."[47]

On July 11, 1953, Salisbury cabled Chancellor of the Exchequer R. A. Butler informing him that a four-power foreign ministers meeting focusing on Germany seemed inevitable. Dulles had changed his mind about the timing of the foreign ministers conference, and now both Dulles and Bidault insisted that this proposed meeting take place before EDC ratification. Dulles's reversal can be attributed both to French pressure and the fact that the West German government had also informally indicated its support for the proposal. Adenauer saw the conference as a way to publicly demonstrate his government's desire to achieve German reunification before the Bundestag elections, which were scheduled for September. Salisbury recommended to the Cabinet that Britain should accept this outcome or risk breaking Western unity, endangering EDC, and hurting Adenauer's chance at reelection.[48] Churchill expressed his objections to Salisbury. The prime minister correctly believed that Dulles and Bidault hoped that any East-West talks would fail, thus making it more likely that the French would ratify the EDC treaty. Churchill did not want to sacrifice the possibility of a summit in a ploy to assure the creation of the EDC. However, he agreed to support a foreign ministers conference, as it seemed unavoidable.[49] Although Salisbury did not press for a summit with the same conviction that the prime minister felt, Churchill did not blame the acting foreign secretary for the outcome of the Washington conference.[50] He did, however, express to Lord Moran his disappointment with the results of the meeting. "They've bitched things up [sic]," Churchill complained.[51]

Unwilling to give up on his summit plan, Churchill cabled Salisbury, who was on board the RMS *Queen Elizabeth*, returning home. The prime minister raised the possibility of appealing again to Washington for a summit to precede the foreign ministers meeting.[52] Salisbury replied, "I am bound to tell you that I am afraid that such a proposal will be quite unacceptable to them." Salisbury said that Dulles had assured him that Eisenhower believed that "it would not be right constitutionally for him as President to be involved in detailed negotiations. . . . You may wish to take account of this in deciding whether or not to send your message." He closed by telling Churchill, "I should add that I found the President, to my surprise, very strongly anti-Russian, far more so than Dulles."[53]

The elderly Churchill exhibited a rapid swing of emotions on the issue of Washington's failure to embrace a summit. At first the prime minister blamed both Eisenhower and Dulles, then he focused his anger exclusively on the secretary of state. On July 18, 1953, he complained to Lord Moran that "apparently Ike is like a king; he cannot deal with detail. There was no nonsense of that sort about Franklin Roosevelt. Of course, Dulles is at the bottom of this." The next day he exclaimed that "Dulles lied when he said Ike did not want to do detail; when I saw him six months ago it was Ike himself who suggested a conference at Stockholm. Of course the Russians may refuse to attend a conference on these terms. They would like me to visit them, I think, to spite America—not that I would ever split from the Americans."[54] Despite Salisbury's warning that the Americans would once again reject a call for a summit, Churchill decided to send his message anyway. It could not have come as a surprise to Churchill when Eisenhower rejected his proposal for the very reasons Salisbury had already outlined.[55]

Perhaps encouraged by the Korean armistice on July 27, 1953, Churchill continuing to believe that a face-to-face meeting between himself and Eisenhower could lead the way to the fulfillment of his dream of détente. In August, Ambassador Aldrich mistakenly told Churchill that Eisenhower contemplated a visit to London. Churchill enthusiastically seized on this idea and wrote immediately to the president. The prime minister promptly received word from Eisenhower that there had been a mistake.[56] Churchill then proposed that the two men meet in the Azores, but the president rejected this idea, citing scheduling problems. Churchill's private secretary Jock Colville believed that "the blunt truth is that E[isenhower] does not want to meet him as he knows he will be confronted with a demand for a conference with the Russians which he is unwilling to accept."[57] These exchanges show that no matter the level of disappointment Churchill felt toward the Americans, he continued to hope that they could be brought around to his way of thinking, particularly if he could talk to Eisenhower face-to-face.

As the dust settled from the Washington conference, Winthrop Aldrich sent a cable to the State Department in which he outlined his views on the state of Anglo-American relations. He claimed that in Britain,

> there has been an increasing apprehension that American foreign policy is over-rigid, formulated without adequate consideration of its impact on our allies and overly responsive to mass emotions in domestic [anti-Communist] political opinion. . . . They fear that what they consider our inflexibility may cause the West to fumble away chances for a settlement with the East.

However, Aldrich concluded that "each nation is given to drawing attention to the mote in the other's eye, and Britain's irascibility occasionally leads them into public opinion extremes which bear little relation to their actual view of the U.S. When the 'chips are down' we can count on the British as allies in the broadest sense of the word."[58] The ambassador's conclusion would prove accurate. Churchill would never push his summit idea to the point of an open breach with Eisenhower. The prime minister might try to cajole or beg Washington into agreement with him, and might be frustrated in the attempt, but he never questioned the value of close ties with America.

THE LONDON FOREIGN MINISTERS CONFERENCE AND BERMUDA

In mid-October 1953 Dulles and Bidault traveled to London for formal talks with Eden, who had recovered and returned to his duties.[59] Dulles also had an occasion to talk informally with Churchill, Eden, and Salisbury at a dinner on October 15, at which talk of a meeting with the Soviets dominated the conversation. Dulles restated Eisenhower's objections to a summit. The president claimed that his duties in Washington precluded his attendance at a lengthy meeting. Moreover, an early summit would be a danger to the ratification of EDC. However, Dulles held out some hope for a summit in the future. He told Churchill that if EDC were ratified, and the Western Alliance thus solidified, then Eisenhower might consider a brief appearance at a four-power meeting.

Apparently this answer did not satisfy Churchill, who then mentioned the possibility that he might go to Moscow alone, or possibly with Eden. The prime minister reminded Dulles that Eisenhower had not objected to this idea when they met in January 1953. He ignored the fact that the president had subsequently advised against Churchill visiting Moscow. An irritated Churchill told Dulles that he could be trusted "not to be entrapped at Moscow." The secretary of state replied that, while Churchill "was of course free to go alone," he would not be functioning in any way as a representative of the United States. Dulles advised Churchill that the public perception of Britain acting as a middleman between Moscow and Washington would "have undesirable effects on our relations elsewhere." Despite Churchill's bluster, the secretary of state reported to Eisenhower "there is every indication that [Eden and Salisbury] do not share Churchill's idea regarding [a] Russian meeting." The two men had, in fact, confided to Dulles their opposition to their prime minister's plan.[60] Despite the opinions held by Washington and his own foreign policy advisers, Churchill's determination to pursue an early summit kept the issue in the forefront of Anglo-American relations.

As a result of the London conference, the West issued an invitation for the Soviets to attend a four-power foreign ministers meeting regarding Germany. When the Soviets rejected the offer, Churchill urged that the once-planned Bermuda meeting be revived. He hoped that a Western summit would be a springboard for an East-West summit.[61] The prime minster expressed elation when Eisenhower agreed. He told Lord Moran, "I put out my paw to Ike, and it was fixed up at once. My stock is very high. There is a feeling that I am the only person who could do anything with Russia." Moran dryly noted in his diary, "What an asset his optimism is! It keeps out the facts. He has set his heart on Moscow, but Ike thinks it can do no good, while Anthony is as certain it will do harm. So Winston has a difficult hand to play."[62] Moran's assessment of the situation proved much clearer than that of the aging prime minister. In fact Eden had already agreed with Dulles that at Bermuda the main goal must be to promote "unity among the three Western Powers in order to counteract centrifugal tendencies in the Western Alliance." The foreign secretary agreed with Washington that if there were to be any negotiations with Moscow, the West needed to develop a firm agenda in advance.[63]

In Washington a State Department internal memorandum noted that "Churchill thinks traditionally in world-wide terms. We should bear in mind that short of appeasement . . . the British are willing to go further than we are in seeking talks with the Russians. The reason for this is largely one of geography (vulnerability to atomic warfare)." The department believed that Churchill was "certain to want to explore thoroughly" his idea of a summit with the Soviets at Bermuda. The memorandum concluded that Churchill could be dissuaded from this course of action if the United States made a persuasive, but not overly rigid, argument against a summit.[64]

Even as Western diplomats were marshaling the arguments against Churchill's summit plan, the Soviets announced that they were willing to discuss the future of Germany and Austria at a four-power conference of foreign ministers. This development gave a further blow to the chances of an East-West summit being held. In the Foreign Office it now seemed that the main agenda at Bermuda would be to prepare for the proposed foreign ministers conference. Foreign Office official Evelyn Shuckburgh noted in his diary, "This may bury Winston's top-level idea even deeper. In fact it may remove his last reason for wanting to stay on as Prime Minister."[65] However, Shuckburgh's assessment would prove to be premature.

Upon his arrival at Bermuda Churchill revived some of the optimism that Moran had noted earlier. The day before the conference formally began, Churchill told Moran that he would attempt to overcome Eisenhower's opposition to a meeting with Malenkov.[66] On December 4, 1953, the president and the prime minister had a private lunch together. Churchill spoke about a possible Soviet summit but assured Eisenhower that he had no intention of being duped by Moscow. Despite his earlier statement to Moran as to his plans, Churchill said he "had no intention of proposing a conference, which would result only in embarrassment and loss of prestige by the Western nations." Eisenhower told Churchill that, while he had not reached a definite decision never to attend a summit, he believed that at the present it would be best not to even mention the idea in public. By keeping public attention focused on a possible top-level meeting, they might delay the French ratification of EDC until such a summit occurred. The prime minister agreed that the best course of action would be for the West to agree to four-power foreign minister talks about Germany and Austria.[67]

True to his word to Eisenhower, at Bermuda Churchill made no formal plea for an East-West summit, instead speaking more generally in favor of détente. However, Eisenhower proved no more hopeful about the idea of improved East-West relations than he had been willing to participate in a summit.[68] As the conference drew to a close Churchill began to realize that Eisenhower would not change his mind.[69] On December 7, 1953, Churchill complained bitterly in private that

> it seems everything is left to Dulles. It appears that the President is no more than a ventriloquist's doll. . . . [Dulles] preaches like a Methodist Minister, and his bloody text is always the same: That nothing but evil can come out of meeting Malenkov. . . . Ten years ago I could have dealt with him. Even now, as it is, I have not been defeated by this bastard. I have been humiliated by my own decay.[70]

Churchill's strange reluctance at Bermuda to press hard on the summit can most probably be attributed to his desire to maintain a solid Western Alliance, and particularly Anglo-American friendship, during a divisive period. Churchill would have hated to find the French and the Americans aligned against his policy of an East-West summit. At his lunch with Churchill on December 4, Eisenhower's noncategorical rejection of an early summit may have convinced the prime minister that he would have to await new developments before pushing Washington for a top-level meeting with Moscow.

THE BERLIN CONFERENCE AND RENEWED HOPE FOR A SUMMIT

During the first half of 1954, East-West relations played themselves out at the Berlin and Geneva Foreign Ministers Conferences. For the most part, talk of a summit receded into the background, but the idea never left Churchill's mind. During the winter of 1954, the prime minister renewed his attempts to convince Eisenhower of the wisdom of holding a summit meeting.

The Berlin Foreign Ministers Conference, which ran from January into February 1954, saw both sides adhering to rather rigid positions. On the question of Germany, the "Eden Plan" summed up the Western position. Reunification could only take place if the Soviets would allow a freely elected, all-German government to join the Western Alliance. The Soviets seemed to be playing for time, hoping to disrupt the creation of the EDC. The one concrete accomplishment at Berlin consisted of an agreement to have a foreign ministers meeting at Geneva to discuss Asian affairs. This conference would include the People's Republic of China as a participant.[71]

While the Berlin meetings were under way, Eisenhower dispatched a letter to Churchill outlining his thinking on the general state of East-West relations. Eisenhower pleaded for Western unity, writing, "More and more I come to the conclusion that the salvation of liberty rests upon the unremitting efforts of all of us to establish a solidarity among ourselves that in major objectives and purposes will remain firm against all assaults . . . you understand these things better than I—in many instances I have absorbed my ideas from you." Contemplating the "disaster for the world" that a Communist victory would entail, Eisenhower wrote of the need "to seek renewed faith in strength from . . . God, and sharpen up his sword for the struggle that cannot possibly be escaped."[72]

Taking his time in responding to Eisenhower's gloomy letter, Churchill did not send a reply until mid-March. The prime minister began by assuring Eisenhower, "There is no difference between us upon the major issues which overhang the world, namely, resistance to Communism, the unity of the free nations, the concentration of the English-speaking world, United Europe and

NATO. All of these will and must increase if we are to come through the anxious years and perhaps decades which lie ahead of hopeful but puzzled man." The prime minister, perhaps to reassure himself, wrote that he understood that the struggle that Eisenhower had alluded to was "spiritual . . . and like me, you still believe that War is not inevitable." Churchill continued with a description of the carnage that would ensue if a hydrogen bomb attack were to be launched on London. He claimed that while the facts about nuclear war were known, most people ignored them. "The reason," he wrote, "is that human minds recoil from the realization of such facts. . . . This merciful numbness cannot be enjoyed by the few men upon whom the supreme responsibility falls. They have to drive their minds forward into these hideous and deadly spheres of thought."

Both the West and the Soviets, he continued,

> are reaching the moment when both sides know enough to outline the doom-laden facts to each other. Of course I recur to my earlier proposal of a personal meeting between Three. Men have to settle with men, no matter how vast, and in part beyond comprehension, the business at hand may be. I can even imagine that a few simple words spoken in the awe which may at once oppress and inspire the speakers might lift this nuclear monster from our world.[73]

Churchill's written plea for a summit was much more eloquent than was his presentation at Bermuda as he sought to turn Eisenhower's mind toward détente by focusing on the horror of nuclear war. Significantly, Churchill's plea for the summit came only after he recounted the vital need for general Anglo-American cooperation in the face of the Soviet Union.

THE WASHINGTON CONFERENCE

Churchill's last great push for a summit meeting came in the spring and summer of 1954 and coincided with the Geneva Conference on Indochina. In April, Churchill proposed that he visit Washington in late May. Eisenhower quickly agreed, stating, "It is high time that we make certain of our common understanding of current and impending events that affect both our countries intimately."[74] The president did not agree to the talks to discuss a summit, but rather to focus on Anglo-American cooperation in Indochina where the French were in danger of a massive defeat at Dien Bien Phu.[75] A few days after his initial message the president cabled Churchill with the suggestion that the meeting be rescheduled so that Dulles could also attend. Eisenhower believed that with the Geneva Conference set to begin on April 26, 1954, it would be helpful to hold an Anglo-American discussion on Indochina.[76]

Churchill and Eisenhower agreed on June 18 as the starting date, with the president urging Churchill to bring Eden along. In his brief survey of the topics that might be discussed, Churchill mentioned nuclear weapons and Indochina but did not list an East-West summit.[77]

When the Geneva Conference continued to drag on, Dulles suggested that the meeting be delayed until June 25, 1954. Eden and Dulles had been at odds over Indochina at Geneva. The Americans disapproved of the British-backed proposal to temporarily neutralize and divide Vietnam until nationwide elections could be held. The secretary of state wanted to avoid the appearance that the Anglo-American talks at Washington were an attempt to repair relations damaged by the disagreements on the fate of Indochina. He would have preferred that a final settlement be reached at Geneva before meeting the British at Washington.[78]

Anthony Eden also expressed his doubts to Churchill about the value of a trip to Washington in the midst of the Geneva Conference. He feared that the Americans would use such a meeting to press the British to intervene militarily to save the French in Vietnam.[79] When Eden did agree to go to Washington, his main focus remained on achieving a peaceful settlement to the war in Indochina and shoring up Anglo-American relations in general. The possibility that Churchill would push for a summit meeting with the Soviets did not appear to enter into his thoughts.[80]

As John Young has pointed out, Churchill concealed his plans to discuss an East-West summit from both the Americans and his own Foreign Office.[81] On the other hand, strong indications existed that he would continue in his search for a summit. On April 27, 1954, Admiral Arthur Radford, chairman of the Joint Chiefs of Staff, met Churchill at Chequers. Radford reported to Dulles that Churchill believed that "the only solution for the problem of containing the Communist offensive, world wide . . . is a personal and intimate conversation between President Eisenhower, Mr. Malenkov, and himself to settle the big problems."[82] Ambassador Aldrich also reported to the State Department that it seemed likely that Churchill would raise the question of a summit meeting at Washington. Despite these warnings, the president made no preparations to parry such a suggestion. Eisenhower confided to his press secretary, James Hagerty, that he had reservations about the meeting but said, "I've decided to let the old man come over for this visit . . . and play it more or less by ear."[83] Eisenhower's major concern centered on strengthening the Anglo-American relationship and proving to the world that the friendship was in good repair. He commented, "The only ones who get comfort out of any troubles we might have would be the enemy."[84]

However, Dulles was more concerned about the informal nature of the talks. On the eve of Churchill's arrival he urged Eisenhower to agree that conversations must not be treated as formal diplomatic agreements unless they were committed to writing. The president concurred, stating, "Winston has a wonderful way of turning conversations at some later time into iron-clad agreements. We surely want to avoid that."[85]

In fact Churchill had very clear goals in mind. The informal nature of the Washington agenda disguised the prime minister's real plans, which he confided to his private secretary, Jock Colville. Colville noted in his diary, on the day of the flight to Washington, that Churchill hoped "to convince the President that we must . . . go and talk to the Russians in an effort to avert war, diminish the effect of the Cold War and procure a ten year period of 'easement' during which we can divert our riches and our scientific knowledge to ends more fruitful than the production of catastrophic weapons."[86]

During the Washington talks, from June 25 to June 29, 1954, the participants discussed a number of topics, including the possibility of RAF planes being outfitted to carry American nuclear bombs, German rearmament, and alternatives to EDC. However, Churchill's chief interest remained the summit.[87] Immediately upon arriving, Churchill and Eisenhower spoke privately. The prime minister expressed surprise and delight when Eisenhower quickly agreed to consider top-level discussions with the Soviets. Eisenhower's only caveat was that the Chinese Communists be excluded from any such talks. Churchill had anticipated that he would have to move step by step to convince the Americans to support a summit. He believed that they would agree only after long discussions on other topics.[88]

At the first formal meeting of the four principal participants, Churchill suggested that a possible East-West summit be added as a topic for consideration. The president then suggested that the vice president and secretary of state might begin a process of high-level talks with the Soviets. If success seemed possible, Eisenhower said he might attend a summit for three or four days. Churchill suggested that he might meet with the Soviets first for an informal "reconnaissance in force" to see if anything promising developed. Conscious of his earlier agreement with Dulles to write down formal decisions, Eisenhower asked the prime minister to write his ideas down for consideration.[89] However, it appears that Churchill never complied with this request.

On the following day, apparently alarmed by Churchill's plan for a solo trip to Moscow, Eisenhower attempted to restrain Churchill's enthusiasm. The president told the prime minister that, while he could not agree to have Churchill travel to the Eastern bloc to meet Malenkov, he would have no objection to a meeting in London or Stockholm. Moreover, Eisenhower insisted that any offer for an East-West summit should be made through the proper diplomatic channels. The president stressed that France should be included in a summit meeting. Churchill also received a warning not to allow Malenkov an opportunity to score a diplomatic victory at an Anglo-Soviet meeting. Churchill replied that he would ask the Soviets to sign an Austrian treaty as a test of their sincerity. Churchill believed that Moscow would welcome this chance to foster better East-West relations.[90] Eisenhower's conversation with Churchill did not dissuade the prime minister from his plan to meet with the Soviets by himself. While he understood more clearly than before that the Americans were not eager for a summit, Churchill viewed Eisenhower's failure to specifically denounce an Anglo-Soviet meeting as an affirmation that he would not object to his "reconnaissance in force."[91]

On June 27 Dulles made his own attempt to stop Churchill from pursuing an East-West summit or an Anglo-Soviet meeting. Dulles reported to Eisenhower, "I pointed out to Mr. Churchill that it was extremely dangerous to have such a meeting unless it would have positive results. An illusion of success would be bad, and also an obvious failure would be bad and might create the impression that the only alternative was war." Dulles told Churchill that if he met alone with the Soviets, the administration would have to publicly state that the prime minister in no way represented the United States. He urged Churchill to consider the matter "very carefully" before making any decision.[92] The official communiqué of the Washington meeting made no mention of a summit meeting beyond some platitudes about holding out "the hand of friendship to any and all nations."[93]

Churchill remained undeterred. He had convinced himself that the Americans had agreed to allow him to meet with the Soviets as a first step toward a three-power summit. Churchill's determination to launch meaningful détente competed only with his desire to cement good Anglo-American relations. He had now reconciled these two objectives to his satisfaction. It is difficult to explain why the Americans did not go further in trying to quell Churchill's summit fever. Klaus Larres argues that Eisenhower "had simply begun to waver a little" on the issue of the summit and Churchill had taken this as a real change of heart on the president's part.[94] John Young suggests that Eisenhower and Dulles were caught off-guard by Churchill's raising of the summit issue at Washington, and assured themselves that he would never follow through on his plan to meet alone with the Soviets.[95] However, it seems hard to believe that Churchill's returning to his favorite international topic surprised the Americans. Knowing Churchill's tenacity, it also appears odd that the Americans would believe he would not go alone to meet Malenkov as a first step to the summit. Perhaps the Americans believed that Churchill was attempting to manipulate them into a three-power summit by threatening an Anglo-Soviet summit that he had no intention of holding. It is also possible that Eisenhower and Dulles hoped that Eden and the Foreign Office would be able to restrain Churchill and thus save a personal confrontation between the prime minister and his American hosts.

Eden and Churchill traveled home on the RMS *Queen Elizabeth*. On this voyage Churchill launched his plan to achieve a summit. The prime minister had convinced himself that Washington would support an overture to Moscow. He explained to Lord Moran, "Ike has crossed a gulf of thought. He has taken a very important step. He has made up his mind that Communism is not something which we must at all costs wipe out, but rather something we have got to learn to live with."[96] Churchill decided to send a personal message to Soviet Foreign Secretary Molotov as soon as possible to inquire about a possible meeting with Premier Malenkov.[97] Eden argued that such an approach to Moscow would cause real damage to Anglo-American relations. However, Eden consented to the message in return for Churchill's promise to resign soon after the meeting took place, leaving Eden as the new prime minister. Churchill also promised Eden that he would first clear the message with the Cabinet. On this point Churchill boldly lied to his foreign secretary. The message went out on July 4, 1954, via London, but Churchill had instructed R. A. Butler to send the message to Molotov without showing it to the Cabinet for comment. The prime minister claimed the message was urgent and, in any case, did not formally commit the Cabinet.[98] On July 5, 1954, Molotov replied that Moscow would look favorably on an official request for a meeting and would treat it as a possible lead-up to a "broader meeting on the highest level."[99]

Churchill must have believed that his long-cherished goal was now in reach. He sent a message to Eisenhower detailing his actions and the favorable reply from Molotov.[100] On July 7, 1954, in a phone conversation between Eisenhower and Dulles, the two men expressed their mutual concern over Churchill's message. The president said that he believed the Soviets agreed to meet Churchill in hopes of causing a breach in the Anglo-American alliance. He told Dulles that if the news broke to the press they would have to distance themselves from Churchill's agenda.[101]

Eisenhower promptly wrote to Churchill informing him how surprised he was at the prime minister's actions. Significantly, Eisenhower, despite his objections, did not ask Churchill to withdraw his invitation to meet Molotov. "You did not let any grass grow under your feet," he began. "When you left here I had thought . . . that you were in an undecided mood about this matter . . . and I would receive some notice if you were going to put your program into action. However, this is now past history and we must hope that the steps you have started will lead to a good result." Eisenhower went on to explain that, if asked by the press, he would say that he disagreed with Churchill's proposal. The president wanted to avoid not only the impression that the

United States supported the meeting but also the alternative interpretation that an Anglo-American rift had prompted Churchill's action.[102]

In a Cabinet meeting on July 7, 1954, Churchill revealed his message to Moscow, and Molotov's reply, to his colleagues. The prime minister stated that Eisenhower had come around to his thinking on détente, at least on the issue of an exploratory Anglo-Soviet summit. Churchill's diplomatic initiative surprised many in the Cabinet, who now demanded that the point of view of the United States be ascertained more fully before the Cabinet backed the idea. Lord Salisbury in particular expressed concern that an overture to Moscow without Washington's consent would be damaging to Anglo-American relations. Eden agreed with Salisbury that no decision should be taken until American, as well as European, opinion on the proposed meeting became clear.[103]

The following day Churchill reported to the Cabinet that Eisenhower had responded in an unsupportive manner to the Molotov message, but the prime minister wanted another chance to change Eisehower's mind. Churchill spent the rest of the meeting explaining to an angry Cabinet why he had not waited to consult them before sending his message to Moscow. In the end, the prime minister received permission to make further inquiries into Eisenhower's state of mind.[104] Churchill cabled Eisenhower, telling him, "I hope you are not vexed with me." The prime minister went on to express his belief that the Soviets would sincerely seek peace to avoid a nuclear war and develop their domestic economy. The cable detailed Churchill's hope that a placated Soviet Union would no longer support Chinese Communist aggression in East Asia. Churchill closed by telling Eisenhower that he would not make an official offer to meet Malenkov until he had heard from Eisenhower.[105]

While focusing his attention on Washington, Churchill faced strong opposition to his proposal from his own colleagues. The Cabinet neared revolt. Lord Salisbury threatened to resign if a summit meeting took place without the United States. The Cabinet demanded that, at the very least, any meeting with Malenkov await the end of the Geneva Conference. The ministers decided that after the conference concluded, if the United States denounced any agreement reached on Indochina, an Anglo-Soviet summit would be out of the question, as it would further worsen relations with Washington.[106]

The next message from Eisenhower to Churchill sounded a much more positive note. "Of course I am not vexed," the president wrote. "Personal trust based upon more than a dozen years of close association and valued friendship may occasionally permit room for amazement but never suspicion. Moreover, I cannot too strongly emphasize to you my prayerful hope that your mission, if you pursue it, may be crowned with complete success." Eisenhower allowed himself some optimism that Moscow might have indeed changed for the better. Perhaps with an eye on events in Geneva, the president stressed the need for Anglo-American cooperation against the threat of aggression from Beijing in Asia.[107] Churchill's reply expressed relief that "no serious differences will arise between our two Governments on account of a Russian excursion . . . by me." He assured Eisenhower that he had no intention of traveling to Moscow, the meeting had to be in a neutral city. The cable did not hide the fact that Churchill hoped that any meeting with the Soviets would lead to a summit that would include the United States, and possibly France. As he had done before, Churchill promised to try to get the Soviets to make a concrete gesture to show sincerity. If the Soviets "vainly" sought to divide London and Washington, he promised to terminate the meeting. He closed by once again asking Eisenhower his opinion before taking formal action.[108]

Eisenhower's cable of July 13 expressed his opinion that "never for one moment would this [meeting] create any difference between two governments which are headed by you and me, or alter in the slightest my profound confidence in your dedication to the principles which have so often united our two nations in time of peril and which today constitute a most precious asset and the best guarantee of peace." The president indicated that, while he could make no guarantees about American public reaction to an Anglo-Soviet summit, he foresaw that it would be viewed as "a noble experiment."[109] The Cabinet, informed of this apparently favorable letter from Eisenhower, demurred on reaching a conclusion until the return of the foreign secretary from Geneva.[110]

With the signing of the Geneva Accords on July 21, the Eisenhower administration changed its tune and tried to convince Churchill not to meet with the Soviets. The agreement on Indochina called for the withdrawal of French troops and the division of Vietnam, with the northern part of the country turned over to the Vietminh. Washington saw the Accords as a victory for Communist aggression and refused to sign the document.[111] Under these circumstances it may have seemed more imperative to the Americans to stop a move by Churchill that would publicly put even more distance between London and Washington on the issue of accommodation with Communism. Eisenhower could not risk being seen to support what his right-wing critics at home would characterize as further "appeasement" by the British.[112]

On July 22 Eisenhower sent a cable to Churchill detailing his continued mistrust of the occupants of the Kremlin. Eisenhower admitted that the world hungered for peace but said he believed Churchill would be disappointed in his attempt to create détente. The president suggested that Churchill switch his agenda from détente to decolonization. The letter stated that if the prime minister sought one last gesture to cement his legacy as a peacetime leader, he should make a major speech promising Western aid for all the colonial peoples in achieving self-determination within a period of twenty-five years or so.[113] Eisenhower's suggestion appears rather naïve, or possibly even insulting. While Washington may have been elated if Britain committed to decolonization, London was by no means prepared to take that step. It is certain that Churchill could not have been pleased with the suggestion that he go down in history as the man who destroyed the British Empire. His lifelong commitment to defending the empire made Churchill an unlikely candidate to accept the role of the liberator of the colonial world.

On the same day as Eisenhower's letter, the prime minister dined with Eden and American Under Secretary of State Walter Bedell Smith in London. Eden had privately urged Bedell Smith to dissuade Churchill from meeting Malenkov, as he refused to listen to his own Cabinet's advice against the idea. At the dinner, Bedell Smith told Churchill that meeting Malenkov would be a mistake as no single Soviet official had filled Stalin's role as undisputed leader. Bedell Smith said that Molotov had more influence in foreign affairs than Malenkov, thereby suggesting that Churchill had seriously misread Soviet politics. Churchill appeared unmoved by the arguments and, perhaps angered over the American's lecture, even suggested that he would travel to Moscow if that was what the Soviets demanded.[114]

Despite the belated signs of American displeasure, and with only the grudging tolerance of Eden, Churchill brought the matter to the Cabinet on Friday, July 23. The stormy meeting ended with the issue deferred until the Monday Cabinet meeting. However, on Sunday, July 26, 1954, the Soviet government issued a call for a European wide conference to discuss the creation of a European security system. Even Churchill had to admit that this was a transparent ploy to disrupt the finalization of EDC. He sent a cable to Moscow withdrawing his offer to meet with Malenkov, saying that the latest Soviet offer "had obviously superseded for the time being the small informal meeting I had suggested." Of course, no dissent arose from the Cabinet.[115]

The end of Churchill's plans to meet Malenkov also ended the possibility of a breach in Anglo-American relations. Of course, even if Churchill did meet with Malenkov by himself, there existed very little possibility that anything more than the public perception of a split between Britain and America would have occurred as it is almost inconceivable that Churchill would have ever made a deal with Moscow that would have ended the Anglo-American alliance. In fact Eisenhower's communications with Churchill in July 1954 demonstrate how anxious he was to reassure the prime minister that he still had faith in Churchill as a loyal ally, even if he disagreed with his summit policy. In addition, Washington probably was anxious not to create another argument, as it already opposed the British position on Indochina. For his part,

Churchill also strove to avoid any quarrel with Washington. In part this can be attributed to the fact that he hoped to quickly arrange a wider summit that would include Eisenhower, and so needed to stay in the president's good graces. Also, Churchill's devotion to what he saw as the "special relationship" between the English-speaking powers would have precluded him from engineering any real break with the United States. Finally, the plan to pursue a summit, while publicly popular, did not have the unreserved support of the Conservative government. Anthony Eden and the Foreign Office held the same cautious view of the summit that prevailed in Washington, and the Americans were well aware of this fact.

AFTERMATH

It must have been a bittersweet experience for Churchill to see his dream of an East-West summit come to fruition only months after he retired in April 1955. By the summer of 1955, the objections of Washington and the Foreign Office to a summit had disappeared. On May 9 the problem of German rearmament and Western solidarity ended with the signing of the Paris Accords that allowed West Germany into NATO as a sovereign state. Only days later, the Soviets signed the Austrian State Treaty that created a free, albeit neutral, Austria. Eisenhower, mollified by these changes in the international situation, agreed to attend an East-West summit meeting in Geneva set for July 1955. In line with Eisenhower's preferred approach to foreign relations, the conference had a set agenda and the Western nations had agreed to a prearranged diplomatic position. It did not resemble Churchill's plan for an informal "man-to-man" discussion. Of course the Geneva Summit produced no important agreements, but Churchill had been able to resurrect the concept of summitry as a tool of diplomacy, after it had fallen out of favor in Western capitals as a result of the Yalta and Potsdam Conferences.[116]

CONCLUSION

Winston Churchill failed in his bid to organize an East-West summit, but that failure was not the result of the strategic weakness of Great Britain. In fact, Churchill's drive for détente demonstrates the importance of Britain in international affairs and in particular London's influence over its powerful American ally. Despite many setbacks and obstacles such as the reluctance of his own Foreign Office and Cabinet, and the resistance of the Eisenhower administration, Churchill clung to his dream. In the summer of 1954 it was only

Moscow's call for a European security conference, which was a blatant ploy to derail Western military cooperation, that forced Churchill to retreat from his planned meeting with Malenkov. Even then, the idea that East-West summitry could be an important tool in reducing the tensions of the Cold War survived Churchill's retirement.

How had Churchill succeeded in keeping his dreams for détente alive, especially in the face of American opposition? Part of the answer lies in the prime minister's personality and heroic stature, but his ability to manipulate the Anglo-American alliance played a major role as well.

Whether one chooses to characterize Churchill as having an indomitable spirit or as being a very stubborn old man, his self-assurance allowed him to persevere when other statesmen would have given up. Winston Churchill certainly had no doubts that Britain had been eclipsed by the United States and the Soviet Union in terms of military and economic strength, but he also had faith that Britain still had a major role to play in international affairs and could yet reverse its relative decline. The prime minister acted on the belief that he could drag an unwilling Eisenhower administration into a summit meeting with the Soviets. Churchill's renown as a hero of the struggle against Hitler and his wartime association with Eisenhower also served him well as he was always treated with respect by the Americans, despite the fact that Eisenhower and Dulles adamantly disagreed with his ideas. Even when Churchill decided to meet Malenkov alone, Eisenhower could not bring himself to treat the prime minister harshly. Given the fact that Washington knew that Churchill did not have the support of the Cabinet, the administration could have taken a much harder line with the prime minister. At worst, if Churchill would not back down, he may have been replaced in a Cabinet revolt by Anthony Eden, whose own ideas on summitry were closer to those of the Americans.

However, the Eisenhower administration's failure to forcefully quell the prime minister's summit plans arose from more than Churchill's doggedness and American respect for the fading statesman's service in the Second World War. Churchill exploited the important position that Great Britain had as the chief American ally in the Cold War. Given that Churchill was one of the firmest supporters of maintaining a "special relationship" between London and Washington, it is odd that Eden and other members of the Cabinet expressed more concern than the prime minister that the summit drive would damage Anglo-American relations. The prime minister was willing to take that risk, secure in his belief that his idea of an easement of the Cold War was the best course of action for Britain and the world as a whole. Churchill also had more faith than his Cabinet colleagues that the Eisenhower administration would not risk an open breach with the United Kingdom, especially over détente: a policy that had so much public appeal in the West. The prime minister's pursuit of détente shows that he was willing to take advantage of the importance of the Anglo-American alliance to Washington by trying to pull the Eisenhower administration into an East-West summit by pushing British policy in that direction. In a reversal of his well-known desire to stay close to the United States, Churchill hoped that to avoid separation from London on the issue of a summit, Washington would to follow his lead. In fact, the Eisenhower administration was most anxious to avoid a public disagreement over East-West relations with London, especially when the question of the integration of West Germany into NATO had not been settled and the West was openly divided over policy on Indochina. Of course, Churchill never would have made a diplomatic break with the United States over the issue of détente. He was too firmly committed to the idea of the "special relationship," and he understood that an East-West summit had to include the United States, but that did not stop him from using Washington's desire not to weaken the Anglo-American alliance to his own advantage.

NOTES

1. John Young, *Winston Churchill's Last Campaign: Britain and the Cold War, 1951–55* (New York, 1996), vi–vii, 7–10; Klaus Larres, *Churchill's Cold War: The Politics of Personal Diplomacy* (New Haven, CT, 2002), xii–xiii, 384–85.
2. Gunter Bischof, "Eisenhower, the Summit, and the Austrian Treaty, 1953–55," in *Eisenhower: A Centenary Assessment*, edited by Stephen Ambrose and Gunter Bischof (Baton Rouge, LA, 1995), 141–46.
3. PRO, FO 800/837, December 13, 1952, Churchill to Eisenhower.
4. FRUS 1952–1954 VI, no. 373, January 8, 1953, memorandum of conversation between Eisenhower and Churchill.
5. PRO, FO 371/106537, January 8, 1953, Colville to the Northern Department; FO 800/821, January 8, 1953, Churchill to Eden and Butler.
6. PRO, FO 371/106537, January 16, 1953, Steel to Mason.
7. PRO FO/371/106537, February 3, 1953, Mason to Steel.
8. Larres, *Churchill's Cold War*, xii–xiii.
9. Larres, *Churchill's Cold War*, 189–90; Young, *Churchill's Last Campaign*, 131–35; Robert Bowie and Richard Immerman, *Waging Peace: How Eisenhower Shaped an Enduring Cold War Strategy* (New York, 1998), 115–16.
10. Lord Moran, *Churchill: Taken from the Diaries of Lord Moran, The Struggle for Survival, 1940–1965* (Boston, 1966), 429.
11. Anthony Eden, *Full Circle* (Boston, 1960), 55–56; Young, *Churchill's Last Campaign*, 136–47.
12. PRO, FO 800/839, March 10, 1953, Churchill to Eisenhower.
13. Bowie and Immerman, *Waging Peace*, 115–16.
14. PRO, PREM 11/422, March 12, 1953, Eisenhower to Churchill.

15. PRO, PREM 11/422, April 5, 1953, Churchill to Eisenhower.
16. PRO, FO 800/821, April 9, 1953, Eisenhower to Churchill.
17. FRUS 1952–1954 VI, no. 396, April 8, 1953, Dulles to Aldrich.
18. PRO, FO 800/821, April 10, 1953, Churchill to Eisenhower.
19. PRO, FO 800/821, April 12, 1953, Eisenhower to Churchill.
20. PRO, FO 800/821, April 12, 1953, Churchill to Eisenhower.
21. PRO, FO 800/821, April 14, 1953, Eisenhower to Churchill.
22. PRO, FO 371/103513, April 17, 1953, Makins to the Foreign Office: text of Eisenhower speech.
23. Bowie and Immerman, *Waging Peace*, 119–21.
24. Martin Gilbert, *Winston S. Churchill*, vol. 8: *"Never Despair, 1945–65"* (Boston, 1988), 816–17.
25. PRO, PREM 11/421, April 21, 1953, Churchill to Eisenhower.
26. PRO, PREM 11/421, April 25, 1953, Eisenhower to Churchill.
27. PRO, CAB 128/26, 29(1), April 28, 1953, Cabinet conclusions.
28. PRO, FO 800/821, May 3, 1953, Foreign Office memorandum by Dixon.
29. PRO, FO 800/821, May 3, 1953, Churchill to Eisenhower.
30. PRO, FO 800/821, May 4, 1953, Foreign Office minute by Strang.
31. PRO, FO 800/821, May 5, 1953, Eisenhower to Churchill.
32. PRO, FO 800/840, May 6, 1953, Churchill to Eisenhower.
33. PRO, FO 800/840, May 8, 1953, Eisenhower to Churchill.
34. Gilbert, *Churchill*, 829–32.
35. John Colville, *The Fringes of Power: 10 Downing Street Diaries, 1939–1955* (New York, 1985), 667.
36. Young, *Churchill's Last Campaign*, 163–64.
37. *Public Papers of the Presidents, 1953*, no. 77, May 14, 1953, president's news conference.
38. FRUS 1952–1954 VI, no. 410, May 12, 1953, Aldrich to the State Department.
39. Young, *Churchill's Last Campaign*, 166–68.
40. Young, *Churchill's Last Campaign*, 179–82.
41. Moran, *The Struggle for Survival*, 435–36.
42. Young, *Churchill's Last Campaign*, 42–42.
43. Memorandum for the Secretary of State, copy of letter from Churchill to Eisenhower, July 3, 1953, Dulles-Herter, box 1, July 1953, Eisenhower's papers as president, Eisenhower Library.
44. PRO, CAB 129/61 C.187 (53), July 3, 1953, Cabinet memorandum by Salisbury.
45. "Washington Talks: Tripartite: Four-Power Meeting with the USSR," State Department lot files, Executive Secretariat, conference files, US-UK-France talks in Washington, July 1953, record group 59, National Archives, College Park, Maryland.
46. PRO, CAB 21/3073, "Visit of Lord Salisbury, Acting Secretary of State for Foreign Affairs to Washington, July 9–15, 1953," July 10, 1953, first tripartite meeting.
47. PRO, CAB 21/3073, "Visit of Lord Salisbury, Acting Secretary of State for Foreign Affairs to Washington, July 9–15, 1953," July 11, 1953, second tripartite meeting.
48. PRO, CAB 21/3073, "Visit of Lord Salisbury, Acting Secretary of State for Foreign Affairs to Washington, July 9–15, 1953," July 11, 1953, Salisbury to Butler; Rolf Steininger, "John Foster Dulles, the European Defense Community, and the

German Question," in *John Foster Dulles and the Diplomacy of the Cold War*, edited by Richard H. Immerman (Princeton, NJ, 1990), 83.

49. Larres, *Churchill's Cold War*, 287; PRO, CAB 21/3073, "Visit of Lord Salisbury, Acting Secretary of State for Foreign Affairs to Washington, July 9–15, 1953," July 12, 1952, Churchill to Salisbury.

50. Moran, *Struggle for Survival*, 464–65.

51. Moran, *Struggle for Survival*, 461.

52. PRO, PREM 11/419, July 16, 1953, Churchill to Salisbury.

53. PRO, PREM 11/419, July 16, 1953, Salisbury to Churchill.

54. Moran, *Struggle for Survival*, 466–67.

55. PRO, PREM 11/419, July 20, 1953, Eisenhower to Churchill.

56. PRO, FO 800/840, August 3, 1953, Churchill to Eisenhower, and FO 800/840, August 8, 1953, Eisenhower to Churchill.

57. Colville, *Fringes of Power*, 679–80.

58. Winthrop Aldrich, American Ambassador to Great Britain, to the Department of State, August 12, 1953, 611.41/8-1253, State Department central files, record group 59, National Archives, College Park, Maryland.

59. Young, *Churchill's Last Campaign*, 213.

60. Dulles to Eisenhower, October 16, 1953, Dulles-Herter, box 1, October 1953, papers of Dwight D. Eisenhower as president, Eisenhower Library.

61. Gilbert, *Churchill*, 909.

62. Moran, *Struggle for Survival*, 529.

63. PRO, PREM 11/418, November 12, 1953, Eden to Dulles.

64. FRUS 1952–1954 V, "Major Meetings with European Leaders," November 16, 1953, memorandum by Director of the Office of British Commonwealth and Northern European Affairs Raynor, 1715–18,

65. Evelyn Shuckburgh, *Descent to Suez: Diaries, 1951–56* (New York, 1986), 110–11.

66. Moran, *Struggle for Survival*, 535–36.

67. Louis Galambos and Daun Van Ee, eds., *The Papers of Dwight David Eisenhower, The Presidency: The Middleway* (Baltimore, 1996), 15, no. 589, diary entry, December 4, 1953.

68. Young, *Churchill's Last Campaign*, 225–26.

69. Moran, *Struggle for Survival*, 539.

70. Gilbert, *Churchill*, 936.

71. Young, *Churchill's Last Campaign*, 238–41, 244–45.

72. FRUS 1952–1954 VI, no. 429, February 9, 1954, Eisenhower to Churchill.

73. FRUS 1952–1954 VI, no. 430, March, no date, 1954, Churchill to Eisenhower.

74. PRO, PREM 11/666, April 22, 1954, Churchill to Eisenhower, and PREM 11/666, April 24, 1954, Eisenhower to Churchill.

75. Larres, *Churchill's Cold War*, 330–31.

76. PRO, PREM 11/666, April 27, 1954, Eisenhower to Churchill.

77. PRO FO 800/841, May 13, 1954, Churchill to Eisenhower, and FO 800/841, May 16, 1954, Churchill to Eden.

78. PRO, FO 800/842, June 9, 1954, Makins to the Foreign Office.

79. PRO, FO 800/842, June 1, 1954, Eden to Churchill.

80. Eden, *Full Circle*, 147–48; Colville, *Fringes of Power*, 691.
81. Young, *Churchill's Last Campaign*, 259.
82. FRUS 1952–1954 VI, no. 439, April 27, 1954, Radford to Dulles.
83. Robert H. Ferrell, ed., *The Diary of James C. Hagerty: Eisenhower in Mid-Course, 1954–55* (Bloomington, 1983), 63–64.
84. Ferrell, *The Diary of James C. Hagerty*, 66.
85. Ferrell, *The Diary of James C. Hagerty*, 72–73.
86. Gilbert, *Churchill*, 996.
87. Young, *Churchill's Last Campaign*, 266.
88. Colville, *Fringes of Power*, 692.
89. FRUS 1952–1954 VI, no. 468, June 25, 1954, memorandum of meeting at the White House.
90. June 26, 1954, Ann Whitman diary series, box 2, papers of Dwight D. Eisenhower as president, Eisenhower Library.
91. Colville, *Fringes of Power*, 693.
92. John Foster Dulles to Dwight Eisenhower, June 28, 1954, Dulles-Herter, box 3, June 1954 (3), papers of Dwight D. Eisenhower as president, Eisenhower Library.
93. FRUS 1952–1954 VI, no. 488, June 29, 1954, declaration by President Eisenhower and Prime Minister Churchill.
94. Larres, *Churchill's Cold War*, 337–39.
95. Young, *Churchill's Last Campaign*, 265, 269–70.
96. Moran, *Struggle for Survival*, 608.
97. PRO, PREM 11/669, July 4, 1954, Churchill to Molotov.
98. Young, *Churchill's Last Campaign*, 271.
99. PRO, PREM 11/669, July 5, 1954, Molotov to Churchill.
100. PRO, FO 800/843, July 7, 1954, Churchill to Eisenhower.
101. Telephone log, July 7, 1954, Dwight D. Eisenhower diary series, box 7, papers of Dwight D. Eisenhower as president, Eisenhower Library.
102. PRO, FO 800/843, July 7, 1954, Eisenhower to Churchill.
103. PRO, CAB 128/27, Cabinet minutes, meeting 47 (4), July 7, 1954.
104. PRO, CAB 128/27, Cabinet minutes, meeting 48 (3), July 8, 1954.
105. PRO, FO 800/823, July 8, 1954, Churchill to Eisenhower.
106. PRO, CAB 128/27, Cabinet minutes, meeting 49 (1), July 9, 1954.
107. PREM, 11/669, July 9, 1954, Eisenhower to Churchill.
108. PREM 11/669, July 9, 1954, Churchill to Eisenhower.
109. PRO, PREM 11/669, July 13, 1954, Eisenhower to Churchill.
110. PRO, CAB 128/27, Cabinet minutes 50 (2), July 13, 1954.
111. Qiang Zhai, *The Dragon, the Lion, and the Eagle: Chinese/British/American Relations, 1949–1958* (Kent, OH, 1994), 138–44, 152.
112. Zhai, *The Dragon, the Lion, and the Eagle*, 148–50.
113. *The Papers of Dwight David Eisenhower* XV, no. 991, July 22, 1954, Eisenhower to Churchill.
114. Walter Bedell Smith to John Foster Dulles, July 26, 1954, international series, box 19, Churchill, July–December 1954 (2), papers of Dwight D. Eisenhower as president, Eisenhower Library.

115. Colville, *Fringes of Power*, 702–3; PRO, FO 800/823, July 22, 1954, Eden to Churchill; Gilbert, *Churchill*, 1036; PRO, FO 800/823, July 26, 1954, Churchill to Molotov.

116. Young, *Churchill's Last Campaign*, 315–18; Larres, *Churchill's Cold War*, 388–89.

Chapter Three

A Struggle for Influence: Arming Iraq

In a May 1953 cable to the Foreign Office, British Ambassador to Iraq Sir John Troutbeck agreed that having the United States assist London in arming Iraq would help to ease the burden on the British military position in the Middle East. "On the other hand," he continued, "I think that the eventual result would probably be that the Americans would replace us here as they have done in Greece. . . . The same thing would happen in other [nonmilitary] fields and Iraq would, I feel sure, soon become as much an American 'preserve' as Greece, and Turkey for that matter, have now become."[1] Troutbeck's fear of growing American influence in Iraq accurately reflected the general sentiment of the British government in regard to Iraq and the Middle East as a whole. This chapter will examine British efforts to protect their interests in Iraq from the perceived threat of American competition as well as from the growth of Iraqi nationalist sentiment.

The United Kingdom's imperial relationship with Iraq began during the First World War when British forces captured the area from the Ottomans. In April 1920 Britain took formal control of Iraq under a League of Nations mandate. Despite sometimes-violent opposition to British rule, London established a pro-British constitutional monarchy for Iraq in June 1921. The British High Commissioner and the new Hashimite king, Faisal I, faced almost continuous nationalist opposition to British control of the country. By the late 1920s, in the face of this pressure, the Iraqi monarchy sought to negotiate an end to the mandate. Anxious to avoid a costly rebellion while still preserving its influence in the country, Britain agreed to the Anglo-Iraqi Treaty of 1930. Under the terms of this treaty, which took effect in 1932, and was to last for twenty-five years, Iraq became a sovereign state but with close ties to Britain. Iraq pledged to seek the advice of Britain in its dealings with foreign countries. A military alliance stipulated that the two nations would cooperate in time of war. In particular, the treaty granted the British the right to use Iraqi ports, railways, and airfields. The agreement called for the Iraqi military to receive its weapons, equipment, and training exclusively from the United Kingdom. Additionally, the treaty allowed the Royal Air Force to continue to operate from two bases in Iraq during peacetime. Despite the end of the formal mandate, Iraqi nationalists correctly saw the Anglo-Iraqi Treaty as a continuation of British domination. But King Faisal and his new prime minister, Nuri al-Said, successfully oversaw the adoption of the treaty.[2]

In June 1941 the British reestablished direct rule over Iraq for the duration of World War II. In the process they deposed the nationalist-minded, pro-Axis prime minister, Rashid Ali. After the war and the reestablishment of full sovereignty, the Iraqi government called for a renegotiation of the Anglo-Iraqi Treaty on a more equal basis. Attlee's Labor government, following its policy of promoting good Anglo-Arab relations whenever possible, quickly agreed to the Iraqi request. In October 1947 the British withdrew all their forces from Iraq except for those manning RAF bases at Habbaniya and Shaiba. Negotiations between the British and Iraqi governments led to the Treaty of Portsmouth in January 1948. By the terms of the treaty the British agreed to return control of the two RAF bases to Iraq while securing the right of reentry in time of war. The British also promised to return control of the railroads and the port of Basra to the Iraqis. The Iraqi military would, however, still be tied to London for equipment and training, and Britain would retain a consultative role in overall Iraqi military planning. In spite of Britain's efforts to appease Iraqi nationalism, Baghdad never ratified the treaty. Iraqi nationalists believed that the treaty made it impossible for Iraq to pursue a truly independent foreign policy. Protesting the agreement, rioting nationalists drove the Iraqi prime minister from power and forced the government to repudiate the proposed treaty.[3]

While the defeat of the Portsmouth Treaty constituted a diplomatic setback for London, the British retained important military and economic interests in Iraq as the Anglo-Iraqi Treaty of 1930 still remained in effect. When Churchill's government was formed in October 1951, Britain's position in Iraq still seemed formidable. The Iraqi Petroleum Company, a British firm, held the oil concession for the country. The two RAF bases were still in British hands. The British controlled the major transportation systems and the port of Basra. British subjects served the Iraqi government as advisers in many fields. An important group of older Iraqi politicians led by Nuri al-Said, as well as the monarchy, supported the continued British presence in their country. This conservative ruling clique was more concerned about the danger of possible Communist expansion into the Middle East than in ending British influence in Iraq.[4] Churchill's government was thus in a position to await a more favorable political climate to try again to replace the Treaty of 1930 with a new agreement that would placate Iraqi nationalists while preserving Britain's interests in the country.

Unlike Britain, in the early 1950s the United States had few ties to Iraq. The Truman administration had acknowledged the dominant role that Britain played in Iraq and had been careful not to undermine its ally.[5] However, American assistance to Iraq was growing, albeit not in an effort to displace Britain. The United States and Iraq concluded a technical assistance agreement in 1951 that promised American advice and aid in agriculture, public health, and general economic development. This program was budgeted at $1,600,000 for fiscal year 1953.[6]

The question of American military aid to Iraq first arose in early 1952 when the British military, anxious to expand the Iraqi army, suggested that America supply some weapons to Baghdad. When the American government subsequently deemed Iraq eligible to buy arms under the Mutual Defense Act of 1949, Washington assumed that the United Kingdom would be grateful.[7] The State Department continued to be respectful of the British predominance in Iraq and instructed the embassy in Baghdad to make it clear to the Iraqis that the United States was not attempting to "supersede the United Kingdom" and would not be competing with London for an arms contract.[8]

Despite the British invitation, and the limited nature of the American offer, the Foreign Office felt compelled to formally restate the British claim to predominance in Iraq and warn the Americans against interference. In November 1952 Britain presented the State Department with an Aide Memoire thanking the Americans for informing the Foreign Office of their offer to sell arms to Iraq and reminding them that the "United Kingdom is the traditional supplier of arms to Iraq." The document went on to state that as more British equipment had become available any American aid "should be kept within very narrow limits."[9] The British concern about limiting American arms supplied to Iraq would continue into the tenure of the Eisenhower administration and provides the core issue of this case study.

IRAQ AND BRITAIN'S POSITION IN THE MIDDLE EAST

The importance of Iraq to British defense planning in the Middle East grew during the years Churchill held office. From 1952 to 1954 the British moved away from earlier plans to send major reinforcements to the Middle East in case of a general war, toward promoting greater military self-reliance among the region's nations. Particularly after the July 1954 Anglo-Egyptian Agreement ended the

British hope of centering regional defense on the massive Suez base, the concept of a Northern Tier position became paramount. If the states that bordered the Soviet Union on its southern frontier could be firmly linked to the West, than the Soviets would be blocked from expanding into the oil-producing regions of the Middle East. Iraq was the key Arab piece of the Northern Tier puzzle, and Britain therefore needed to promote good relations with Baghdad to secure its cooperation in a regional defense pact.[10] A defensive alliance that could be financially supported by the United States, but politically dominated by London, also constituted a major element of Eden's plan to maintain Britain's power in the Middle East.

In early 1953, Permanent Under Secretary of State for Foreign Affairs Sir William Strang outlined the state of Anglo-Iraqi relations to Churchill. Strang informed the prime minister that the Anglo-Iraqi Treaty of 1930 had been open to revision since October 1952. The permanent under secretary believed that Baghdad would most likely ask for the return of the air bases at Habbaniya and Shaiba but that the Foreign Office and the Chiefs of Staff were hoping to continue to have some access to the bases.[11] A February 1953 internal memorandum by the Foreign Office further outlined the major goals for Britain in Iraq. The first goal consisted of ensuring that Britain "continue to enjoy as large a proportion as possible of the military facilities granted under the 1930 Treaty." The second goal was more economic than strategic in that the Foreign Office wanted to protect the Iraqi Petroleum Company from any threat of nationalization and defend the interest of any other threatened British firms.[12]

The British government saw a military connection as the key link to continued close association with Baghdad. On February 7, 1953, T. C. Rapp, of the British Middle East Office, cabled Ambassador Troutbeck with an analysis of the strategic requirements of Anglo-Iraqi relations. The telegram assumed that it would be impossible for the United Kingdom to maintain ownership of the air bases in Iraq if Egypt, as expected, took control of the Suez base. This being the case, Rapp proposed that the United Kingdom find "a modified yet useful position in Iraq . . . under the guise of helping in building up the Iraqi armed forces [which] will yet enable us to build up defense in support of our strategy."[13] In March 1953, when Nuri al-Said, now acting as Iraqi defense minister, suggested that the Anglo-Iraqi Treaty of 1930 should be modified, London expressed no surprise and prepared to accept renegotiating with an eye toward promoting long-term good relations with Iraq.[14] Despite the challenge posed by Arab nationalism in the early 1950s, London was clearly determined to maintain its valuable political and economic interests in Iraq.

THE ROOTS OF THE ARMS CONTROVERSY

The somewhat reluctant growth of the influence of the United States in Iraq complicated Britain's plans to remain the dominant foreign power in Baghdad. In January 1953 American Ambassador Burton Y. Berry suggested to Secretary of State John Foster Dulles that the United States offer a grant of military aid to Iraq so that Baghdad would not have to divert money from internal development to purchase weapons. Berry informed Dulles that while Iraq could afford to pay for sufficient arms for internal security, it would need assistance to properly play a role in regional defense. Berry acknowledged that because of the Anglo-Iraqi Treaty of 1930, the United Kingdom would have to be consulted, but apparently he believed that Britain did not possess the resources to fully equip Iraq.[15] However, at this point, Dulles did not share Berry's enthusiasm for providing arms to Iraq. The secretary of state informed the ambassador that due to heavy military commitments in Korea and Europe, the United States had few resources to spare for the Middle East. Dulles suggested to Berry that in order to quell Iraqi fears of the Soviets, Baghdad should be encouraged to join a regional defense pact that would include a Western power.[16] In the early part of 1953 American interest in Iraq remained limited due to other commitments, but Baghdad soon sought to involve Washington more deeply in its own plans to expand the Iraqi military.

In February 1953, at a meeting with the military attachés of both the United States and Great Britain, Nuri al-Said began to put pressure on the West for arms. Nuri stated that he "was not satisfied with the policies of the British and United States governments in furnishing equipment and supplies." Nuri expressed a desire for the most modern arms available and claimed that Iraq could pay for these arms, although dollars were in short supply. Ambassador Berry saw this meeting as a pointed reminder to Britain that Iraq would seek arms elsewhere if not satisfied with those purchased from London.[17]

Iraq also expressed interest in receiving grants of military aid from the West. On March 22, 1953, Iraqi Foreign Minister Taufik Suwaidi gave letters to the British and American ambassadors outlining Iraq's need for assistance from both countries. Suwaidi explained that, as Iraq hoped to build up her forces to four army divisions, it could not afford to pay both for military expansion and internal development. In an interview with Troutbeck, Suwaidi also made it clear that Iraq sought a modification of the 1930 Treaty that would hand the air bases back to Iraq. Troutbeck stood firm on both issues. He told the Iraqi foreign minister that he "did not see how we could effectively help Iraq in war unless we had the right to maintain RAF squadrons actually stationed in Iraq." On the issue of military aid, Troutbeck warned

Suwaidi that because of Britain's tight financial position, Iraq should not count on "obtaining gifts" from London.[18]

Despite his cool response to the Iraqis, in communication with his own government Troutbeck urged London to carefully consider the matter. The ambassador believed that Iraq had a sincere determination to face up to the Soviets and therefore hoped to forge closer ties to the West. Troutbeck believed that as the West continually urged the "free world" to arm itself against Communist aggression, Britain and the United States had an obligation to consider Iraq's request. He foresaw Great Britain supplying most of the arms to Iraq, with the United States granting financial aid to allow for the purchase of additional weapons to fill in any gaps. Troutbeck also suspected that the Iraqis would be more pliable in renegotiating the 1930 Treaty if they were granted aid.[19]

Two days later in a meeting between Nuri and Troutbeck, the Iraqis told the British that if London was having financial troubles, Iraq would seek assistance from the United States. Nuri pointed out that Iraq was being treated differently from Turkey. While it was true that Baghdad had not yet agreed to join the proposed Middle East Defense Organization, or any other regional alliance, Turkey had received military aid from the West long before it joined NATO. Nuri repeated Suwaidi's call for an end to the stationing of British forces in Iraq during peacetime.[20] The following evening Nuri changed tactics from bluster to bribery when he again spoke to Troutbeck. Nuri told the ambassador that if Great Britain proved able to assist Iraq in expanding its armed forces, than Baghdad might be able to allow Britain to continue to use military facilities in Iraq.[21]

At the same time as they were applying pressure to the British, the Iraqis were also seeking assistance from the United States. When Foreign Minister Suwaidi met with American Ambassador Berry on March 22, 1953, he stressed the importance of Iraq to the West in terms of its oil reserves and strategic location. Berry expressed concern that in November 1952 the United States had offered reimbursable military aid to Iraq but had received no reply. Suwaidi countered that, while Baghdad would probably accept this offer, Iraq needed a grant of aid to speed up the rearmament process. The foreign minister claimed that if Iraq diverted money from economic development to arms, "Communism would arise in Iraq." Berry's initial report to the State Department of the Iraqi request for aid did not include a recommendation as to action, but he expressed pleasure that Iraq was taking the Communist threat seriously and seemed willing to participate in a regional defense pact.[22]

On March 26, 1953, Ambassador Troutbeck discussed the Iraqi request with American Chargé d'Affaires Philip Ireland. The ambassador tried to convince Ireland that Baghdad was not contemplating weakening its ties to

Britain. He claimed that the Iraqis expected to receive arms from Britain and only required funding from the United States.[23] Two days later Nuri had a private conversation with Ireland in which he contradicted Troutbeck. According to Ireland, Nuri's "approach differed from that described by the British Ambassador. Nuri emphasized to me his wish for the best arms possible. If American tanks were better than British he wanted them; similarly with planes, etc." When pressed about the possibility of accepting the November 1952 offer to purchase American arms, Nuri replied that this would be politically impossible because of the negative impact such expenditures would have on economic development. Mirroring his earlier complaints to Troutbeck, Nuri said that he could not understand why Iraq was expected to pay for weapons while Turkey received them free of charge. He claimed that Iraq held a strategic position just as valuable as Turkey, particularly with Iran in an unstable state.[24]

The Iraqi government was clearly hoping to exploit its strategic importance in order to force the West to provide it with military aid. Nuri also seemed quite willing to play the British against the Americans in an effort to get the best possible deal for Iraq. In doing so, Iraq forced the British to face up to the conundrum of their desire to have the United States assist them in holding the Middle East for the West and their fear that America might replace them as the dominant foreign power in the region.

BRITAIN AND THE UNITED STATES RESPOND TO THE IRAQI REQUEST

The Foreign Office considered a number of factors in its analysis of the Iraqi request for military assistance. The British and Iraqis already had a long-term plan to expand the Iraqi armed forces. Two Iraqi divisions had already been reequipped. Phase II of the plan called for the equipping of a third division, with Phase III to include additional expansion of Baghdad's forces. London saw the present Iraqi call for aid as an attempt to accelerate Phase III with the infusion of money from America and Britain. London believed that Baghdad was using Western fear of the Soviet Union to extract grants from the West even though Iraq probably had the capacity to pay for military expansion with its own resources. Still the Foreign Office believed that Britain and the United States should be generally sympathetic to Iraq's desire for a better-prepared military, which would be a valuable addition to regional security. While Iraq seemed unsure about what shape a regional pact should take, it was still allied to the British by the Anglo-Iraqi Treaty and Britain remained hopeful that the two vital air bases would continue to be used by the RAF.

In Whitehall, the fact that for the first time Iraq had requested assistance from the United States raised the specter of a potential rival in Baghdad. Therefore, the Foreign Office believed that the next step should be consultation with the Americans. After apprising the United States on the extent of current Anglo-Iraqi plans for rearmament, London hoped to get Washington to agree to a number of points of cooperation. Due to the Treaty of 1930, and the fact that in any war Iraqi forces would be fighting side-by-side with British units, London wanted Iraq to continue to be armed exclusively with British pattern weapons. On this point the Foreign Office noted that the United States already appeared to agree in principle. London also wanted to make sure that any Anglo-American moves to rearm Iraq were publicly linked to a policy of fostering an anti-Soviet military alliance in the Middle East. Lastly, the Foreign Office hoped that the United States would agree that Iraq should be asked to pay for military expansion, as a gradual buildup was not only affordable but also prudent, given the low level of training in the Iraqi army.[25]

The British Treasury expressed particular concern that Iraq not be given a gift of free arms from London as the government had cut the overall British defense budget. The Treasury suggested that if Iraq could not pay for weapons it would have to get them from the United States or arrange for Washington to "procure UK arms offshore for supply to her."[26] Ambassador Troutbeck, however, disagreed; he warned the Foreign Office that if Iraq were forced to pay for military expansion, it would indeed curtail its economic development, which "would have unfortunate political repercussions here."[27]

London partially accepted Troutbeck's assessment but still hoped that Iraqi oil revenues might lead to a surplus in the development budget that could be shifted to the purchase of arms. The Foreign Office instructed Sir Roger Makins, British ambassador to Washington, to inform the State Department that while it was possible that Iraq would not be able to purchase all the arms it required, there remained a need to assess how much it could afford.[28] One of the reasons that London proved willing to give Iraq some benefit of the doubt on its ability to pay for weapons was its concern for the future of Anglo-Iraqi relations after renegotiation of the 1930 Treaty. An April 10, 1953, internal Foreign Office memorandum noted that

> it will be difficult to dress up any new agreement in such a way as to enable the Iraqi government to show that they have achieved their national aspirations while at the same time ensuring that we secure our minimum requirements. It therefore seems that any new arrangement to be acceptable to the Iraqis may need to be less precise than the present Treaty. To compensate for this we should develop the direct military liaison with the Iraqis, which is proving so successful at present.[29]

Whitehall's careful analysis of the situation delayed a response to Baghdad. It was not until June 22, 1953, that Troutbeck delivered London's ambiguous answer to the Iraqi request for arms. Britain expressed support for Iraq's goal of an expanded military and claimed to be willing to live up to its treaty obligations to assist Iraq. However, London said it "would only consider further assistance as part of the regional defense problem." Troutbeck stressed that this did not mean that Britain believed that the bilateral alliance of 1930 should be scrapped until a firm plan was found for its successful replacement. Furthermore, Britain wanted to help insure that Iraqi oil revenues would allow both internal development and military expansion to take place simultaneously. When Nuri al-Said renewed the Iraqi request for a grant of arms later in the summer, Troutbeck told him that it would be impossible to fulfill his request. As Troutbeck explained, the United Kingdom had many bilateral and multilateral military alliances and could not afford to set a precedent by giving arms to Iraq, as its other allies would then demand similar grants.[30]

As London decided not to grant aid to Baghdad, Iraqi pressure on the United States for arms aid increased. In May 1953, Secretary of State Dulles stopped in Baghdad as part of a tour of the Middle East. In meetings with Dulles, Nuri and other Iraqi officials reemphasized the strategic importance of Iraq vis-à-vis the Soviet Union and stressed the danger to domestic security of diverting funds from internal development. The Iraqis expressed disappointment that the United States had given assistance to Saudi Arabia, Pakistan, and Iran but not to Iraq. Dulles expressed satisfaction that the Iraqis recognized the danger that Communism and the Soviet Union posed to the Middle East, but he informed the Iraqis that he could not give a definitive answer to their request for aid.[31]

Although Dulles would not give a positive response to the Iraqis while in Baghdad, he came away with the impression that Iraq was the Arab state most concerned with the Soviet threat.[32] Despite his favorable impression, Dulles still resisted answering Iraq's request. On June 10, 1953, he cabled the American Embassy in Baghdad with instructions that the Iraqis should be told that, while Washington had not yet prepared a definitive reply, their "request is receiving careful consideration and it is hoped that mutually satisfactory arrangements can be reached at an early date." Additionally, Dulles wanted Baghdad to know that Congress and the Eisenhower administration would look more favorably on its request for arms if Iraq were a member of a regional defense pact.[33]

Ambassador Berry gave his analysis of the situation to the State Department in two cables on July 14, 1953. According to Berry, the Iraqis were reluctant to settle for reimbursable aid, as the United States had earlier proposed, because they feared this would set a dangerous precedent by which they might be permanently denied grant aid for military expansion. Berry cautiously endorsed Baghdad's call for a military grant. The ambassador also warned Washington that it could not expect Iraq to join a Western-led regional security pact for the time being because of the growing influence of Arab nationalism. However, Berry argued, the current regime in Baghdad showed a willingness to cooperate with the West "to a reasonable degree" and should thus be supported in its goal of military expansion. An expanded Iraqi army would also serve as a valuable prop for Iraq's pro-Western government in its struggle against internal critics. Berry recommended that an Anglo-American committee be established to study Iraq's defense needs and financial resources and formulate a joint military aid program.[34]

In August, Berry continued his argument for extending grant aid to Iraq. The ambassador reasoned that the recent Western-backed coup in Iran, which had overthrown the nationalist Prime Minister Mohammed Mossadegh and returned the pro-Western Shah to power, made the time ripe for the United States to reap the maximum political benefit from a generous grant to Iraq. Berry expressed the opinion that the United States would gain the most political influence by furnishing American equipment for a completely new unit of the Iraqi army, such as a mountain brigade, which the Iraqis were proposing to raise. Financial assistance to purchase British weapons or equipment, which would be scattered throughout the Iraqi military, would not represent "tangible evidence" of American concern for Iraq as well as would a full brigade visibly supplied by Washington's largesse.[35]

In September 1953, State Department and Department of Defense officials traveled to Baghdad to meet with the embassy staff for face-to-face discussions about the question of aid. Alexander Daspit outlined the thinking of the Joint Chiefs of Staff and the State Department at the initial meeting. According to Daspit, the Joint Chiefs had in the past opposed military aid to the Middle East as unjustified "in the context of the world-wide politico-military situation." The Pentagon also wanted a Middle East Defense Organization, or some other regional alliance, in place before supplying arms to the Arabs. This stance had changed under pressure from the State Department. Assistant Secretary of State for Near Eastern Affairs Henry Byroade had proposed that all pro-Western governments in the Middle East should be strengthened through aid regardless of current defense arrangements. In August, the American Chiefs of Diplomatic Missions for the Middle East had met in Cairo and suggested that Iraq be given aid in the amount of $8 million to $12 million. The fact that Dulles advocated a strong Northern Tier defensive pact also influenced the military's thinking. It demonstrated that the State Department shared the long-term goal of creating a regional alliance. By the fall of 1953 the Joint Chiefs considered bilateral aid to friendly Arab states as a positive interim step on the road to regional defense.

Now that the Pentagon and the State Department were in agreement that Iraq should receive aid, the details needed to be discussed with the embassy personnel. The Baghdad meeting of September 3, 1953, demonstrated that American officials differed in their opinion as to how the United States should treat the British connection to Iraq. Colonel Sievers presented the Department of Defense's thinking at the meeting. Sievers said that after the formal establishment of a bilateral agreement with the Iraqis, the United States would begin to supply American arms, although Baghdad would be expected to pay for as much of the equipment as possible. Embassy staff members pointed out that the British-equipped Iraqi army was meant to operate as a corps of the British army during wartime and would therefore probably want American aid to be used for the offshore procurement of weapons from the United Kingdom. Colonel Sievers demurred, stating his belief that Congress and the administration would not look favorably on the idea of using the British as an intermediary for the supply of aid to Iraq. With the exception of Ambassador Berry, the Baghdad Embassy diplomats remained unconvinced that only American arms should be supplied to Iraq. However, all the participants agreed that there was "some merit" to the ambassador's plan to offer to equip a single unit with American weapons.

Mr. Barrow, political officer of the embassy, raised the issue of cooperation with the United Kingdom. Barrow said that he assumed that the United States planned to continue to recognize the British as the principal arms supplier to Iraq and would only supply equipment unavailable from London. Everyone at the meeting agreed that coordination with the British was essential, but Colonel Sievers argued against having "the British participate directly in determining how our dollars and our equipment would be utilized."

In a further conversation between Barrow and Alexander Daspit, the former noted that the British Embassy had expressed concern about the prospect of the United States undermining Britain's relationship with Iraq by offering to supply arms to the Iraqis gratis, while the United Kingdom still required payment from Baghdad. Daspit replied that London must have already considered this and reconciled itself to an American grant program for Iraq.[36]

The embassy staff in general seemed more concerned with the sensitivities of London than did the visiting officials from Washington. In a cover letter to the Office of Near Eastern Affairs that accompanied the official record of the September 3 meeting, Chargé d'Affaires Philip Ireland reiterated to the State Department the embassy's concerns that the British were very uneasy about the possibility of the United States supplying arms to Iraq.[37]

At this point the American military seemed determined to supply American-made weapons to Iraq in order to demonstrate clearly the source of the grant. They did not believe that American aid should be tailored to fit the needs of Great Britain. The Pentagon expressed little concern for Britain's position in

Iraq. On the other hand, some of the State Department officials at the embassy showed a much greater sensitivity to British concerns about competition from the United States and more of a willingness to cooperate with London.

BRITAIN'S GROWING FEAR OF AMERICAN RIVALRY

The State Department's assessment of the level of Britain's fears proved accurate. In particular, British Ambassador Sir John Troutbeck harbored apprehensions about the expansion of American influence in Iraq. The ambassador considered the presence in Iraq of American technicians as a threat to Britain's commercial predominance even before the issue of arming Baghdad had come to the fore. Troutbeck disliked the American civilian advisers in Iraq, describing them as combining "an instinctive distrust of British 'imperialism' with a firm conviction of the superiority of American methods and machines as well as a pronounced inclination to 'empire-build' on their own." The ambassador realized, however, that there was little that the United Kingdom could do to stop American penetration if Iraq requested it, especially since London hoped to maintain good relations with both Baghdad and Washington.[38]

Troutbeck's conversations with the American ambassador following Iraq's request for arms from both nations only fueled his suspicions. In May 1953 Berry described to Troutbeck his own experience in Greece. He admitted that once the American military mission arrived the British were "pushed . . . out." This caused, Berry said, understandable resentment on the part of both the Greeks and the British. The American ambassador adopted a sympathetic stance to the British position in Iraq, at least in Troutbeck's presence. But Her Majesty's ambassador was left with the impression that America would eventually drive the British out of Iraq. Troutbeck's fears were magnified when Berry confided to him that the Iraqis had asked the United States to pressure the British to give up the air bases at Habbaniya and Shaiba, a move which would involve Washington in the renegotiation of the 1930 Treaty.[39] In his annual political summary of 1953, sent to Foreign Secretary Eden, the ambassador concluded that "there is a grave danger lest by a combination of free gifts and a blundering diplomacy the Americans will end up seriously weakening our own position without getting very much out of it either for themselves or for the free world in general."[40]

The Eastern Department of the Foreign Office agreed with Troutbeck's ominous assessment of American penetration in Iraq. The risk of being replaced by the United States, not only in Iraq, but all over the Middle East, greatly disturbed London. However, the Foreign Office recognized that, as Britain needed American assistance to resist the Soviet Union in the region, the risk of being displaced by their ally had to be accepted. As far as the threat posed by the possibility of American weapons being given to Iraq, the Foreign Office believed that the "best hope" for Britain lay in maintaining a close military relationship with Baghdad along the lines of the 1930 Treaty, and in the possibility that American aid would not amount to much.[41]

London's best chance to remain the dominant foreign power in Iraq lay in getting the United States to cooperate in limiting the scope of its own aid to Iraq. The Foreign Office now faced the task of bringing London's concern to the attention of the Eisenhower administration.

ANGLO-AMERICAN NEGOTIATIONS

Discussions and negotiations between the United States and Great Britain concerning the issue of arms supplies to Iraq began even before Washington made the formal decision to grant Baghdad's request. In July 1953, the State Department made an effort to assuage Britain's fears in a letter given to the British Embassy. The letter reassured London that, despite the Iraqi request for American aid, the United States still recognized that Britain held the position of principal supplier of arms to Baghdad. America also recognized the value of maintaining the Anglo-Iraqi Treaty as the best method of Western cooperation with Iraq until a regional pact could be created. The State Department offered to hold informal discussions with Britain about the general issue of Iraqi-Western relations.[42] Foreign Office officials concluded that talks with the United States would be valuable in terms of making it clear that Britain did not intend to withdraw from its "special position in Iraq."[43]

The Foreign Office instructed Sir Roger Makins to inform the Americans that London was pleased that Washington shared its view that Iraq should be chiefly supplied with British weapons. In London's opinion the best method of funneling American aid to Iraq was through the offshore purchase of arms from the United Kingdom. Makins's instructions also made it clear that the United States should be firmly warned against establishing any military mission in Iraq. The Foreign Office expressed concern that an American military team would disrupt the Anglo-Iraqi military relationship. London expected Makins to make clear to the State Department that the British considered their current close ties with Iraq's military as the foundation of their political relationship with Baghdad, a relationship that Britain deemed vital to maintain because the strategic position of the West in the Middle East rested heavily on retaining the base facilities in Iraq.[44] The British Chiefs of Staff fully concurred with the views of the Foreign Office.[45]

In an early September 1953 meeting with Makins, Henry Byroade informally notified the ambassador of the State Department's decision to propose that Iraq be granted approximately $10 million in military assistance. Byroade also told Makins that despite London's wishes, under the legal authorization for this grant, the United States would have to send a military team to supervise its expenditure. In an attempt to placate Makins, Byroade said that this military group would not constitute a "military mission in the proper sense of the term."[46]

The British were especially sensitive about the issue of American military advisers. From London's point of view, the American military seemed to have no desire to protect British interests in Iraq. Reports of conversations between British military personnel and American officers touring the Middle East indicated that the Pentagon seemed anxious to supply American weapons to Iraq, possibly to a separate unit. The American army officers, while agreeing that the overall British plan for the Iraqi military should not be disrupted, did not see any value in the United States supplying only nonlethal aid to the Iraqi army. The Foreign Office realized that while this was the first American foray into supplying arms to the Arabs, it would probably not be the last. London thus hoped to control, as much as possible, American entry into the field.[47] In addition, Ambassador Troutbeck warned that Baghdad might seek to exploit any perceived Anglo-American rivalry. If Iraq could get free arms from the United States, Troutbeck speculated that they would no longer be willing to purchase British weapons.[48]

In late November 1953, once the preliminary discussions were over, the Foreign Office prepared a brief to be used in negotiations with the United States. While the United Kingdom welcomed American contributions to the defense of Iraq and the Middle East as a whole, the Foreign Office sought to remind Washington that a plan already existed for the equipping of the Iraqi armed forces with British weapons. The special relationship that London had with Iraq, as outlined in the Anglo-Iraqi Treaty of 1930, made it the responsibility of the United Kingdom to provide Iraq with all necessary arms and training. The establishment of a rival American military mission in Iraq would tend to reduce Iraqi confidence in London and thus endanger the status of the valuable RAF bases in the country. Furthermore, if Iraq purchased American weapons, it would not only violate the 1930 Treaty but also drain valuable dollar reserves from a member of the Sterling Area. The brief suggested that the United States be urged to provide aid for Iraq through the offshore purchase of British arms. London wanted any direct American aid to be limited to construction material, vehicles, or ammunition. The Americans were to have no role in equipping or training the Iraqi air force. Finally, the Foreign Office wanted to ensure that the Americans made it clear to Baghdad that no rivalry existed between London and Washington and that any American aid would simply be complementary to that of Britain.[49]

Foreign Secretary Eden forwarded this memo to Makins along with a pared-down list of "principal objectives." Eden wished "to ensure that the grant of US military aid . . . does not conflict with the efforts being made by HMG to build up the Iraqi armed forces or otherwise injure British interests in Iraq." Makins was instructed to dissuade the United States from sending "any form of military mission or advisory group to Iraq." Finally, Eden sought to convince the Americans to use offshore purchases of British arms as their primary method of granting aid to Iraq. If Washington insisted on sending some equipment, it would be far preferable that it be in the form of vehicles, not weapons.[50]

That same November the State Department prepared its own brief to use in the upcoming talks with the British. The document contained a number of important points and was, in general, close to the British position. The State Department recognized the special position that Britain had in Iraq, and the Middle East as a whole, and wished to avoid disrupting that position. With this in mind, Washington would agree to follow the British plan for Iraqi rearmament, as it constituted a part of the overall British defensive scheme for the Middle East. While the United States normally only provided military assistance that could readily be identified as American equipment, in the case of Iraq it would agree to consider the use of offshore purchases of British equipment "to a reasonable extent." However, some areas of assistance would have to be mutually agreed to that would allow some distinctly American equipment to be deployed. Lastly, due to the 1930 Treaty, the United States would not seek to place a training mission in Iraq, but it wanted to accept some Iraqi candidates for training in American military schools.[51]

On December 3, 1953, serious negotiations began in Washington involving the British Embassy and representatives of the Departments of State and Defense. The Americans said that they recognized that in any Soviet invasion of Iraq, British and Iraqi forces would be on the front lines together and thus should retain standardized weapons. The Americans also acknowledged that the strength of the Anglo-Iraqi relationship was the key to maintaining the air bases at Habbaniya and Shaiba. However, at this first meeting the Americans were less congenial on the details of the supply of assistance. The British perception that the U.S. military was more anxious to promote American influence in Iraq than the State Department proved true. Possibly under pressure from the Pentagon, the State Department's original draft of November 1953 was ignored. Makins reported to Eden that the Americans "displayed little interest in the possibilities of off-shore procurement in the United Kingdom." The Americans also reminded the British that federal law required the United States to send a Military Assistance Advisory Group (MAAG) to Iraq if Baghdad received any military aid, although the MAAG would not have to have a formal training role. The Pentagon's Colonel Sievers continued to press the idea of the United States equipping a complete Iraqi unit. While disappointed with the American stance, Makins agreed to prepare a draft statement of principles to discuss at the next meeting.[52]

The British ambassador suggested to London that it would have to back down on some of the goals that Eden had set for the negotiations. According to Makins, the stationing of an American MAAG should not be resisted, although it should be made clear that the British retained the responsibility for general training of the Iraqi forces. The British could try to maintain control over the grant through close cooperation with the Americans in Iraq. As far as offshore procurement of arms, Makins believed that Washington should only be asked to "give favorable consideration" to the idea.[53]

In Whitehall, Makins's tepid draft proposal sparked debate as to the next move by London. The British military outlined the stark choices. The first would be to allow the negotiations to continue on their current path, which would lead to Iraq becoming "an American sphere of influence." The second would be to deny Washington the right to supply arms to Iraq under the terms of the Anglo-Iraqi Treaty. The Foreign Office believed that the latter course of action would prove unwise for a number of reasons. If London were to press too hard on the matter, the United States might abandon the whole idea of assisting in the defense of the Middle East. Alternately, they might ignore Britain's concerns and proceed directly with negotiations for aid with Baghdad. If the Iraqis were made aware of the fact that Britain had attempted to limit American aid, it would have a detrimental effect on Anglo-Iraqi relations. The Foreign Office developed a consensus that, as American aid could not be blocked altogether, the best the United Kingdom could hope for was to strengthen Makins's draft proposal so that it came into line with the original Foreign Office draft that Eden had sent to him in late November.[54]

On December 28, 1953, Makins presented to the Americans the original Foreign Office draft of November as the official British proposal. Makins received a pleasant surprise when the discussions resumed on December 30, 1953. The hard line taken by the Americans in the December 3, 1953, Washington meeting had receded, and now the Americans presented the British with a draft agreement that was identical to the State Department's much more agreeable internal draft of November. Between the December 3 and the December 30 meeting the Department of Defense had softened its stance. While the Pentagon had strongly objected to the British proposal that the Iraqi air force should be totally off-limits to American aid, it had otherwise dropped its objection to offshore purchase and its demand to arm an entire unit of the Iraqi army.[55]

With the Americans seeming to give way, London tried to press its advantage. On January 13, 1954, Makins received a cable from Eden instructing him to try to get the State Department to agree to all of the British demands. In the opinion of Whitehall, the United Kingdom had already made a major concession to the Americans before the negotiations began by allowing them any role in equipping the Iraqi army. The Foreign Office expressed disappointment that the United States continued to demand the right to allow Iraqi officers to train in the United States. London also hoped to retain exclusive responsibility for the Iraqi air force. If the Americans felt compelled by law to send a MAAG, Eden at least wanted to approve all the instructions Washington gave to the military team. Eden reminded Makins that Britain still had full military responsibility in the Middle East and the insertion of limited American aid did not change this fact. American interference would, moreover, weaken the political position of the United Kingdom in Baghdad and thus tend to jeopardize the entire Western position in the Middle East.[56]

This line of argument did not impress Her Majesty's ambassador to Washington. In his reply to Eden on January 14, 1954, Makins made a strong appeal for accepting the current American proposals:

> I recognize that the draft . . . does not give us all we want, and it would no doubt be possible to obtain some small improvement by further negotiation. I am, however, reluctant to approach the State Department on the basis of your telegram . . . which seems to be based on the belief that our bargaining position in this matter is stronger that it appears to be. . . . Even if we were to obtain an agreement . . . this would be done at the cost of sacrificing the mutual confidence that would be essential to the satisfactory operation of the agreement in practice. . . . I venture, in conclusion, to underline my view that the surest way to defeat our object in this matter is to let the Americans think that we have no confidence in them.[57]

Eden replied to Makins that he did not lack faith in the United States. The Foreign Secretary reiterated the claim that British control of aid to Iraq offered benefits to the West as a whole, not just Britain. According to Eden's cable,

> The point is rather that we regard their policy of offering aid 'without strings', and unaccompanied by any US commitment for the defense of the area as tending to weaken our hold on the strategic facilities which we enjoy under the Anglo-Iraqi Treaty, which the American planners wish to share and which is in the general Western interest that we should retain.

As a point of compromise, however, Eden expressed a willingness to retract the demand that London approve the instructions to the American MAAG.[58]

In further negotiations, Assistant Secretary of State Henry Byroade assured Makins that the United States had no serious interest in "supplying or training" the Iraqi air force but objected to being excluded from doing so on principle.

As for the training of a small number of Iraqi army officers in American military schools, Byroade argued that this might be necessary to familiarize them with any non-British pattern equipment supplied.[59] By mid-February 1954 the Foreign Office had come to the conclusion that the Americans would not easily back down on these issues. Whitehall decided to accept the American terms and proceed to a formal agreement. London had been placated by informal American assurances "to safeguard [Britain's] position in practice, at least for the present." Another factor in London's acceptance of the agreement was a fear that the Iraqis would find out that the United Kingdom had tried to prevent Baghdad from receiving American aid.[60]

On February 26, 1954, the United States and the United Kingdom initialed a Memorandum of Understanding that detailed their agreement over the supply of American military aid to Iraq. Both governments agreed to keep the agreement secret. The key components of the Memorandum of Understanding were as follows: All American aid would fit into the current Anglo-Iraqi expansion plan. The United States agreed to "impress upon the Iraqi government" that any American training or aid should be considered supplementary to that of Britain. Washington agreed to consider the use of offshore procurement to allow the Iraqi army to retain its compatibility with British forces. While the United States still hoped to provide some equipment that could be readily identified as American, it would consult with London about the nature of that aid. London had to concede the rights of the Americans to accept some Iraqi officers for training in the United States and to send a MAAG to Iraq, but Washington agreed to close consultation on these matters. To allow the agreement to conform to the Anglo-Iraqi Treaty of 1930, the United Kingdom formally waived those parts of the treaty that barred Iraq from obtaining non-British arms and training.[61]

The Memorandum of Understanding went a long way toward meeting the demands that London had to limit the nature of American aid to Iraq. It is clear that the State Department meant to do everything practical to avoid disruption of the Anglo-Iraqi relationship. Despite the evident American willingness to cooperate, Eden had been reluctant to make any compromise. The British remained suspicious of the United States and seemed upset that they found themselves in a position to have to accept any American involvement in Iraq, even if the need for American aid arose in part from Britain's own limited financial resources.

U.S. INTEREST IN THE NORTHERN TIER

While the British continued to harbor concerns that the United States would supplant them in Iraq, Washington seemed to have been much more concerned about promoting regional security than in replacing Britain as the dominant power in Iraq. In January 1954 the Eisenhower administration had decided to furnish military aid to Pakistan in order to facilitate ongoing Turko-Pakistani talks about the formation of a mutual defense pact. Turkey and Pakistan successfully concluded an alliance in April 1954. Washington saw this as the beginning of a wider Northern Tier pact that it hoped would eventually include Iraq.[62]

The American aid package to Iraq was meant to promote the idea of a Northern Tier alliance. When President Eisenhower wrote to the chairman of the House Committee on Armed Services to formally request the aid package for Iraq, he stressed Iraq's regional importance as "strategically located in the Northern Tier of countries between the Soviet Union and the heart of the Middle East."[63] The State Department also hoped that the military aid to Iraq would spur Baghdad to join with other nations of the region in a mutual security pact. In late January 1954 Ambassador Berry received an update on the status of Washington's plans to arm Iraq. The State Department instructed him to stress to Baghdad, when the time came for a formal announcement, that the level of aid it received would be based in part on Iraqi willingness to join Turkey and Pakistan in a defensive alliance.[64]

The Iraqi government found itself in an awkward position. Nuri al-Said had privately informed Berry that Iraq had an interest in adhering to the Turko-Pakistani pact but Arab nationalists, in particular those in the Egyptian regime, opposed any Arab state joining a non-Arab security organization. In order to placate Arab nationalists at home and abroad, at least temporarily, Iraq disavowed any intention of receiving American aid or joining the Turko-Pakistani alliance at the April 1954 meeting of the Arab League.[65]

Secretary of State Dulles expressed his extreme displeasure with Baghdad's announcement in a cable to Berry. "It seems to us that if the Iraqis are so unwilling to stand up and be counted on [the] side of the free world," Dulles wrote, "we should reflect very carefully before concluding [the arms] agreement." Dulles stated that if Baghdad had a legitimate fear about the public reaction to receiving American weapons, then it would not be worth pushing the issue. He concluded that

> our whole policy regarding military assistance to the Middle East is based on [the] concept of collective security and while we have been willing to consider military aid to Iraq without insisting upon adherence to any regional defense pact . . . we have been counting upon at least clear-cut public recognition by Iraq of her interest in regional defense against outside aggression and her willingness to cooperate with other states who also see the danger."[66]

Although Berry believed that Iraq should not be pressured into joining any regional alliance that it did not feel comfortable with, he duly informed Iraqi

Prime Minister Jamali of Dulles's concerns. Jamali assured Berry that the communiqué issued from the Arab League meeting did not truly reflect Baghdad's position. The prime minister said that Iraq remained interested in American aid and would adhere to the Turko-Pakistani pact "at the proper time."[67]

Dulles and Eisenhower discussed the issue at a meeting in Augusta, Georgia, on April 19, 1954. The two agreed "it was all right to conclude the mutual security agreement with Iraq on the condition that the actual aid given should be dependent upon the international situation at the time." Both men hoped that by offering aid to Iraq, despite Baghdad's public statements, they would achieve their ultimate goal of having Iraq join with Turkey and Pakistan.[68] Berry received instructions that same day to inform the Iraqis that wording would have to be inserted into the aid agreement stating that the United States would take "into account the international position in the [area] in determining the amount, character, and timing of aid."[69] The formal Military Assistance Treaty was signed on April 21, 1954, and on April 25 the Iraqi government publicly announced that the United States would supply "the Iraqi army with military assistance without any conditions or obligations either political or pertaining to alliances."[70]

Washington's desire to promote a defensive pact in the Middle East provides one explanation for its willingness to so closely cooperate with the British in Iraq. The United Kingdom already had a viable military relationship with Baghdad, and London also supported regional defense. To replace Britain in Iraq would be costly and counterproductive. In the early 1950s the Eisenhower administration still considered the Middle East to be principally a British sphere of influence, with London holding the area for the West as a whole.

CONTINUED BRITISH SUSPICION OF AMERICAN MOTIVES

The signing of the Anglo-American Memorandum of Understanding, which had been kept secret from Baghdad, and the acceptance by Iraq of American military aid did not completely settle the issue for London. Despite Washington's efforts to cooperate with London, the British remained fearful that American involvement in Iraq would undermine their own position.

When the American Military Assistance Survey Team visited Iraq in May 1954 to assess the needs of the Iraqi military, the British were kept well informed of its progress. The head of the team, Brigadier General Harry Meyers, met with the British ambassador and military attaché.[71] However, not all interaction between British and American officers proved as cordial. At a dinner party in June 1954 the new American military attaché to Baghdad, Lt. Colonel Tucker, expressed a negative attitude about Britain's role in the Middle East to the commander of British Middle East Land Forces, Brigadier T. E. Williams. Tucker said that the British had made a "mess" of the Middle East and the United States would have to help Britain "put it right." Tucker claimed that the Iraqis loathed the British and looked to America to help them oust the United Kingdom. The colonel expressed amazement that London required the Iraqis to pay for military equipment which, he believed, was of inferior quality. When challenged by Williams to prove his allegation about the British material Tucker backed down, saying his information came second-hand from junior Iraqi officers.[72]

The British Embassy in Baghdad tried to play down Tucker's comments. The embassy reported to the Foreign Office that the colonel's intemperate statements were due to his naïveté, and possibly the ill effects of excessive drinking at the party. On the whole, the embassy judged that relations between the American and British militaries had improved over the past months. However, the impression remained that the American officers were "holding back from any real cooperation with us on instructions from above."[73]

During the summer of 1954 the Foreign Office continued to have a high level of anxiety about the American involvement in Iraq, as well as a belief that, at present, little could be done to change the situation. According to a Foreign Office minute prepared on June 30, "despite the lip service which the United States government pay to the predominant position of the United Kingdom in Iraq, they cannot but diminish the British position." While the Foreign Office acknowledged that the American diplomats in Baghdad were not working "actively against our interests," it appeared that neither were they cooperating to the extent that the Memorandum of Understanding would allow. The Foreign Office believed that the supply of free equipment by the United States, regardless of the motivation, tended to weaken the Anglo-Iraqi military links. The paper concluded that

> the increase of American activity in Iraq postulates a corresponding decrease of British standing. . . . There appears to be no remedy to this situation until and unless the economic position of the United Kingdom permits us to play a role comparable to that of the USA. The object of this paper is therefore to bring home the fact that encouragement by Her Majesty's Government . . . of the US initiative in Iraq and neighboring countries, even though the official policy of the US Government is to maintain the Anglo-Iraqi connection, will nevertheless tend to weaken rather than strengthen the British position in Iraq and render more difficult the conclusion of an eventual understanding with the Iraqi Government.[74]

Another major concern of London centered on the possibility that Iraq would continue to play the United Kingdom against the United States for its own advantage. When British Under Secretary for Middle Eastern Affairs

Evelyn Shuckburgh visited Baghdad in November 1954, Nuri al-Said told him that Iraq could not afford to pay for the weapons needed to expand its army. According to Nuri, the United States seemed willing to provide Iraq with tanks and aircraft. While the Iraqis would prefer to continue to use British pattern weapons, they would have to accept free American weapons rather than purchase arms from London. In Ambassador Troutbeck's assessment, Nuri believed that he had "an opportunity of squeezing both us and America and forcing us to pay the maximum price for building up the Iraqi forces. . . . The Iraqis are past masters of playing us and the Americans off against each other. This is the first thing we must avoid."[75] Sir Roger Makins subsequently received instructions from London to warn the United States government not to accept the Iraqi plea of poverty and to stick to the Anglo-American Memorandum of Understanding that left Britain as the primary arms supplier to Baghdad.[76]

In December 1954, Sir John Troutbeck's final report as ambassador to Iraq painted a fairly grim picture for Anthony Eden. Troutbeck admitted that in principle the United States had agreed to support Britain, but he believed that

> no Englishman living in Iraq can remain unmoved when he sees hordes of American experts sweeping into a country whose traditional ties are to ourselves and hears them denigrating all that Britain has done in the past and is attempting to do at the present. . . . There is also a big question mark as to the significance of American military aid. Is it really meant to be complementary to British activity in the same field, or is the aim to push us to a minor role?

The ambassador went on to state that there did not appear to be an easy solution to the British dilemma in Iraq:

> There is, I think, no doubt that—our relative positions in the world being what they now are—we must accept, and accept with a good grace, an increase of American influence in this part of the world. . . . At the same time we can legitimately do our best to defend our position. . . . We can also feel legitimate doubts as to whether or not the Americans are going about matters in the right way. If they were wittingly or unwittingly to destroy our traditional hold in Iraq, could they take our place? It seems doubtful. . . . There is therefore a serious danger that the Americans may end up destroying the British bulwark and leave nothing but a vacuum for communism to fill.

Troutbeck concluded that, while the United Kingdom needed to avoid a diplomatic break with the United States that would only serve the ends of the Soviet Union, it had to redouble its efforts to maintain its economic and military relationship with Iraq.[77]

Prime Minister Churchill and Foreign Secretary Eden shared Troutbeck's determination to maintain Great Britain's traditional position in Iraq.[78] The foreign secretary hoped that the renegotiation of the Anglo-Iraqi Treaty in the form of a regional defense pact would be the key to cementing British influence in Baghdad. Accordingly London concluded a new Anglo-Iraqi Special Agreement in March 1955. This new bilateral accord was to come into effect when Britain adhered to the alliance that Turkey and Iraq had previously signed in February 1955. This three-way alliance was formalized by the creation of the Baghdad pact in April 1955. This defensive agreement linked the United Kingdom to both Ankara and Baghdad. London hoped that by replacing the Treaty of 1930 with a regional defense arrangement, nationalist feelings in Iraq would be quelled. In order to conclude the new Anglo-Iraqi Special Agreement, Britain had agreed to hand over sovereignty of the much-valued air bases within a year, although they would be available for use by the RAF in case of a war.[79]

However, Eden's plan to preserve British power in Iraq would not work if the Iraqi government came to rely on the United States as its principal arms supplier. Once Britain had turned over control of the air bases, the future of the Anglo-Iraqi relationship centered on military cooperation, and therefore, London had to remain Baghdad's primary Western military ally. The new British ambassador to Baghdad, Sir Michael Wright, made it clear to London that if Britain hoped to successfully maintain its position in Iraq, then London would have to agree to Baghdad's continued requests for free weapons. If London could not supply a considerable grant of arms, then Baghdad might well turn to the United States as its benefactor.[80]

Following a suggestion by Wright, the Foreign Office decided that Iraq should be supplied with de facto free weapons by granting Baghdad financial credit in lieu of demanding payment for handing over the permanent installations at the Habbaniya and Shaiba bases. As part of the Anglo-Iraqi agreement, Baghdad had agreed to pay London for the RAF facilities at the air bases. Under the proposed plan this payment would not have to be made if Iraq promised to use the money it saved to purchase arms in the United Kingdom. The Foreign Office had come to the conclusion that, even if the United States could be made to agree to supply Iraq's arms demands solely through the off-shore purchase of British weapons, this would eventually lead to Washington becoming the "the guiding influence with the Iraqi forces." Under Secretary for Middle Eastern Affairs Evelyn Shuckburgh believed that Britain could only maintain its influence in Baghdad, and some control over American aid to Iraq, if it could prove that it could make a considerable contribution of free arms itself.[81]

As might be expected, the British Treasury objected to the proposed plan to trade arms for the air base facilities. Concerned with the tight financial position of Britain, the Treasury did not wish to establish a precedent of giving grant aid to British allies. The Treasury also expressed concerns that it would be embarrassing to attempt to argue with Baghdad that British facilities in Iraq were worth less than it might seem, in order to limit the amount of the grant, while at the same time attempting to get Egypt to pay as much as possible for the transfer of the Suez facilities.[82]

Despite the financial concerns, Eden presented the Cabinet with the proposal on March 14, 1955. The Foreign Secretary informed his colleagues that

> the United States is already giving military assistance to Iraq on a limited scale. If we are to maintain our position in Iraq . . . I think that we must make a similar contribution. If the Iraqi forces are not equipped with the same equipment as our own forces, the lines of communication and supply in war would be liable to break down. We are already concerned at American attempts to supplant us in this field. In spite of our present understanding with the United States that the Iraqi forces should continue to look primarily to the United Kingdom for equipment and training, we must expect these attempts to continue. We cannot resist them effectively as long as the arms they supply are free, while ours have to be paid for.[83]

The Cabinet approved the scheme on March 15, 1955, and the Working Party on Anglo-Iraqi Negotiations formally endorsed the base facilities for arms deal a short time later.[84] The final arrangements with Iraq were not made until December 1955, by which time Eden had ascended from the post of foreign secretary to that of prime minister. Under the terms of the Anglo-Iraqi Special Agreement, Baghdad had agreed to pay £2,750,000 for the permanent installations at Habbaniya, Shaiba, and the port of Basra. In diplomatic notes exchanged on December 20, London agreed to waive this payment in return for an Iraqi promise to spend the sum on weapons and training from the United Kingdom.[85]

During Eden's term in office, the United Kingdom continued to defend its position as principal arms supplier to Iraq. The suspicion that London maintained toward the United States led to some minor squabbles over the supply of arms. Secretary of State Dulles complained in private to other American officials that Eden seemed to be more concerned with defending the British monopoly on arms supply than he was with ensuring that Iraq had the weapons it needed to contribute to regional defense. In general, however, the United States continued to support London's position by supplying Iraq with weapons purchased offshore in Britain and by abiding by the terms of the Memorandum of Understanding.[86]

The competition between the United Kingdom and the United States came to an abrupt end in 1958. In July of that year nationalist army officers overthrew the monarchy and killed the king and Nuri al-Said. Soon afterward the new Iraqi government withdrew from the Baghdad pact, terminated military and civilian aid programs from the West, and began to receive military assistance from the Soviet Union. If an Anglo-American rivalry for influence in Baghdad had ever existed, the Iraqis had now rendered it a moot point.[87]

CONCLUSION

This case study demonstrates how Great Britain exploited the value of its position in the Middle East as an asset in containing the Soviet Union in order to maintain some of its empire in the region. The weakness of the British economy made it difficult for London to finance the military buildup of the pro-British regime in Baghdad to the level that the Iraqis wanted. Baghdad's invitation for American participation in its armament program directly challenged British domination of Iraq. However, Britain successfully defended its predominance in Iraq from the possibility that the United States would replace it as Baghdad's chief Western ally. Of course, the fact that the Eisenhower administration had no desire to replace the British in Iraq made that task fairly easy. In Iraq, the convergence of Washington's Cold War aims with London's imperial aims aided the British position. However, this chapter also reveals some of the underlying difficulties that Britain faced in trying to remain a global power.

The evidence makes clear that the Eisenhower administration did not intend to use arms grants to Iraq to supplant Britain's predominant influence in that country. In fact Washington actively cooperated with London in defending British influence in Iraq. In the Memorandum of Understanding of February 1954 the State Department not only agreed to formally recognize Britain's position in Iraq but also to allow London a great deal of say in how American aid would be allocated. The State Department successfully resisted the more aggressive stance of the American military on the issue of supplying a complete Iraqi unit with American arms. By agreeing to some offshore purchase of British equipment, the United States not only helped to keep Iraq armed with British pattern weapons but also put money into the British treasury. While the United States did have expanding civilian contacts with Baghdad, Eisenhower and Dulles seemed mostly concerned that Iraq be drawn into a regional, anti-Soviet military agreement. American aid would only be forthcoming, they warned Baghdad, if Iraq would fulfill a role as a member of a Northern Tier pact. The United States cannot be accused of subsequently trying to dominate the Baghdad Pact, as Dulles resolutely refused to join that alliance despite the desires of London. The pattern of American actions during the course of its military grants to Iraq show that Washington remained primarily concerned with the Soviet threat to the region, not to the expansion of

American influence. Of course, America's deference to the primacy of Great Britain in Iraq served Washington's goals of containing the Soviet Union with as little expense as possible.

The Eisenhower administration's cooperation with Churchill's government meant that Baghdad had to continue to look to London as its main foreign ally, thus reinforcing British influence in Iraq. However, even after the signing of the Memorandum of Understanding, the British remained anxious that the Americans would replace them in Iraq, even if Washington did not intend for this to happen. The level of London's concern about American rivalry shows that Britain's plan to hold onto its Middle Eastern empire had some inherent weaknesses.

Churchill's government sought to induce more American interest in the Middle East in order to protect its own imperial interests. London hoped that the United States would finance an anti-Communist regional security organization that Britain would politically dominate. Anxious for American aid in the Middle East, London could not treat America simply as an imperial rival and seek to fully exclude them from Iraq. Therefore, London found itself trapped in a dilemma. As soon as Washington agreed to supply some free equipment to Baghdad, however limited by agreement with London, the British had to compete with American largesse. The United States, while not attempting to replace Britain, became a potential rival in the Middle East because of its far greater wealth. The Iraqi government clearly understood that by threatening to turn to America as a source of free arms, it could compel London to stop demanding payment for all the weapons it supplied to Baghdad. A conservative monarchy like Iraq could safely play the Western powers against each other instead of making a possibly dangerous approach to the Soviet Union for military aid. The fact that London sought to renegotiate the Anglo-Iraqi Treaty of 1930, in order to preserve its traditional position in Iraq, also strengthened Baghdad's bargaining position. In the end, despite protests by the exchequer, Eden had to agree to supply arms in exchange for the RAF base facilities.

London understood that its strategy of drawing Washington into greater involvement in the Middle East was a dangerous game. Anxious to fight the Cold War in the Middle East, Washington was willing to help in creating a regional security pact, but London feared that the Americans might unwillingly destroy Britain's empire in the region by becoming the dominant outside power. In Iraq, Churchill's government played the game the best it could. London directed, and limited, American penetration of Iraq and reorganized its own relations with the country by forming the Baghdad Pact. Britain's victory was short-lived, as the nationalist revolt in 1958 severed Iraq's ties with the West, but London's diplomatic achievements show the resiliency of the British Empire during Churchill's peacetime government.

NOTES

1. PRO, FO 371/104238, May 29, 1953, Troutbeck to Bowker.

2. Phebe Marr, *The Modern History of Iraq* (Boulder, CO, 1985), 29–51.

3. Marr, *Modern History of Iraq*, 82–87, 101–4; David Devereaux, *The Formulation of British Defense Policy Towards the Middle East, 1948–58* (New York, 1990), 7–8.

4. Marr, *Modern History of Iraq*, 110; Waldemar J. Gallman, *Iraq under General Nuri: My Recollections of Nuri al-Said, 1954–1958* (Baltimore, 1964), 172–74; Elizabeth Monroe, *Britain's Moment in the Middle East, 1914–1971* (Baltimore, 1981), 154.

5. Ritchie Ovendale, *Britain, the United States and the Transfer of Power in the Middle East, 1945–1962* (New York, 1996), 26.

6. United States Embassy in Baghdad to the Department of State, May 7, 1953; 611.87/5–753, State Department central files, record group 59, National Archives, College Park, Maryland.

7. Devereaux, *British Defense Policy*, 142–43.

8. FRUS 1952–1954 IX, no. 1385, October 24, 1952, Acting Secretary of State to Embassy in Baghdad.

9. FRUS 1952–1954 IX, no. 1387, November 7, 1952, the British Embassy to the State Department: Aide Memoire.

10. Devereaux, *British Defense Policy*, 120; Steven Freiberger, *Dawn Over Suez: The Rise of American Power in the Middle East, 1953–1957* (Chicago, 1992), 85–86.

11. PRO, FO 371/104678, March 12, 1953, Strang to Churchill.

12. PRO, FO 371/104678, February 10, 1953, Foreign Office minute by Rhodes.

13. PRO, FO 371/104678, February 7, 1953, Rapp to Troutbeck.

14. PRO, FO 371/104236, March 4, 1953, Troutbeck to Foreign Office; March 7, 1953, minute by Rhodes on Troutbeck cable.

15. Burton Berry, Ambassador to Iraq, to John Foster Dulles, Secretary of State, January 10, 1953, 787.5-MSP/1-1053, State Department central files, record group 59, National Archives, College Park, Maryland.

16. FRUS 1952–1954 IX, no.122, March 6, 1953, Secretary of State to Embassy in Iraq.

17. Burton Berry, ambassador to Iraq, to the State Department, Feburary 14, 1953, 787.5/2-1453, State Department central files, record group 59, National Archives, College Park, Maryland.

18. PRO, FO 371/104236, March 22, 1953, Troutbeck to Eden.

19. PRO, FO 371/104236, March 24, 1953, Troutbeck to the Foreign Office.

20. PRO, FO 371/104236, March 24, 1953, Troutbeck to the Foreign Office.

21. PRO, FO 371/104236, March 25, 1953, Troutbeck to the Foreign Office.

22. FRUS, 1952–1954 IX, no. 124, March 22, 1953, Berry to the State Department.

23. FRUS, 1952–1954 IX, no. 1389, March 26, 1953, Ireland to the State Department.

24. FRUS, 1952–1954 IX, no. 126, March 28, 1953, Ireland to the State Department.

25. PRO, FO 371/104235, April 2, 1953, Foreign Office minute by Baker.

26. PRO, FO 371/104236, April 14, 1953, Bancroft to Ross.

27. PRO, FO 371/104237, April 24, 1953, Troutbeck to the Foreign Office.

28. PRO, FO 371/104237, May 15, 1953, Foreign Office to British Embassy, Washington.

29. PRO, FO 371/104680, April 10, 1953, Foreign Office minute by Ross.

30. PRO, FO 371/104187, week of June 24, 1953, British Middle East Office weekly summary to Eastern Department, Foreign Office; FO 371/104238, July 14, 1953, Bromley to Ross.

31. FRUS 1952–1954 IX, no. 32, May 18, 1953, memo of conversation; FRUS 1952–1954 IX, no. 33, May 18, 1953, memo of conversation.

32. 147th meeting of the National Security Council, June 1, 1953, NSC series, papers of Dwight D. Eisenhower as president, 1953–1961, Eisenhower Library.

33. FRUS, 1952–1954 IX, no. 1392, June 10, 1953, Dulles to the American Embassy in Iraq.

34. Burton Berry, ambassador to Iraq, to the Department of State, July 14, 1953, 787.00/7-1453 and 787.5-MSP/7-1453, State Department central files, record group 59, National Archives, College Park, Maryland.

35. FRUS 1952–1954 IX, no. 1395, August 24, 1953, Berry to the Department of State.

36. FRUS 1952–1954 IX, no. 1396, September 3, 1953, memorandum of conversation at the American Embassy, Baghdad.

37. Philip W. Ireland, Chargé d'Affairs to Iraq, to Parker T. Hart, Director of the Office of Near Eastern Affairs, September 9, 1953, 787.5-MSP 9-953, State Department central files, record group 59, National Archives, College Park, Maryland.

38. PRO, FO 371/111016, April 8, 1954, British Embassy in Iraq to Eden.

39. PRO, FO 371/104238, May 29, 1953, Troutbeck to Bowker; FO 371/104680, November 24, 1953, Troutbeck to Allen.

40. PRO, FO 371/110986, January 11, 1954, Troutbeck to Eden.

41. PRO, FO 371/104238, June 13, 1953, minute by Powell-Jones on May 29, 1953; letter from Troutbeck to Bowker.

42. PRO, FO 371/104238, July 8, 1953, Beeley to Ross, including copy of July 1, 1953, letter from the Department of State.

43. PRO, FO 371/104238, August 6, 1953, Foreign Office minute by Falla.

44. PRO, FO 371/104240, August 29, 1953, Foreign Office to Embassy in Washington.

45. PRO, DEFE 4/64, September 3, 1953, Chiefs of Staff Committee, 102nd meeting, item 1.

46. PRO, FO 371/104240, September 9, 1953, Makins to the Foreign Office.

47. PRO, FO 371/104240, October 8, 1953, Foreign Office minute by Powell-Jones.

48. PRO, DEFE 5/50, October 30, 1953, Troutbeck to the Foreign Office, copy sent to Chiefs of Staff Committee.

49. PRO, FO 371/104241, November 26, 1953, Foreign Office memorandum "United States Military Aid to Iraq."

50. PRO, FO 371/104241, November 27, 1953, Eden to Makins.

51. FRUS 1952–1954 IX, no. 1398, November 25, 1953, Dulles to the American Embassy in Iraq.

52. PRO, FO 371/104241, December 3, 1953, Makins to the Foreign Office.

53. PRO, PREM 11/1895, December 3, 1953, Makins to the Foreign Office.

54. PRO, FO 371/104241, December 7, 1953, Foreign Office memorandum by Powell-Jones; December 7, 1953, Foreign Office memorandum by Falla; December 8, 1953, memorandum by Allen.

55. PRO, FO 371/104241, December 30, 1953, Makins to the Foreign Office, including text American statement of "US Military Aid to Iraq"; Henry Byroade, Near Eastern Affairs to Deputy Under Secretary of Defense Robert Murphy, Jan. 5, 1953, 787.5MSP/1-554, State Department central files, record group 59, National Archives, College Park, Maryland.

56. PRO, PREM 11/1895, January 13, 1954, Foreign Office to Makins.

57. PRO, PREM 11/1895, January 14, 1954, Makins to the Foreign Office.

58. PRO, PREM 11/1895, January 20, 1953, Foreign Office to Makins.

59. PRO, PREM 11/1895, January 21, 1953, Makins to the Foreign Office.

60. PRO, DEFE 5/51, February 16, 1954, Falla to the Chiefs of Staff Committee.

61. FRUS, 1952–1954 IX, no. 1407, February 26, 1954, memorandum of understanding between the governments of the United States and the United Kingdom.

62. Freiberger, *Dawn Over Suez*, 89–90.

63. Dwight D. Eisenhower to Dewey Short, chairman, Committee on Armed Services, House of Representatives, January 26, 1954, box 37, Mutual Security and Assistance, 1954 (1), Subject series, confidential file, White House central files, Eisenhower Library.

64. FRUS 1952–1954 IX, no. 186, January 28, 1954, acting secretary of state to American Embassy in Baghdad.

65. Freiberger, *Dawn Over Suez*, 91–92.

66. John Foster Dulles, secretary of state, to the United States Embassy in Baghdad, April 8, 1954, 787.5 MSP/4-854, State Department central files, record group 59, National Archives, College Park, Maryland.

67. FRUS 1952–1954 IX, no. 1411, April 16, 1954, Berry to the Department of State; no. 1412, April 18, 1954, Berry to the Department of State.

68. Memorandum of conference between Dwight D. Eisenhower and John Foster Dulles, April 19, 1954, box 1, Meetings with the President, 1954 (3), White House Memo series, John Foster Dulles Papers, Eisenhower Library.

69. FRUS 1952–1954 IX, no. 1413, April 19, 1954, Dulles to the United States Embassy in Iraq.

70. Burton Berry, ambassador to Iraq, to John Foster Dulles, secretary of state, April 25, 1954, 787.5 MSP/4-2554, State Department central files, record group 59, National Archives, College Park, Maryland.

71. Arthur B. Allen, second secretary of United States Embassy, Iraq, to the Department of State, June 1, 1954, 787.5-MSP/6-154, State Department central files, record group 59, National Archives, College Park, Maryland.

72. PRO, FO 371/111053, June 29, 1954, War Office to the Foreign Office.

73. PRO, FO 371/111053, July 14, 1954, Hooper to Brewis.

74. PRO, FO 371/110998, June 30, 1954, Foreign Office minute by Hooper.

75. PRO, PREM 11/1895, November 6, 1954, Troutbeck to the Foreign Office.

76. PRO, PREM 11/1895, November 18, 1954, Foreign Office to Makins.

77. PRO, PREM 11/1408, December 20, 1954, Troutbeck to Eden.

78. PRO, PREM 11/1408, December 23, 1953, Churchill to Eden.

79. Anthony Eden, *Full Circle* (Boston, 1960), 243–44; PRO, FO 31/115754, March 31, 1955, "Text of the Special Agreement between the United Kingdom and Iraq initialed in Baghdad on the 30th of March, 1955."

80. PRO, PREM 11/1408, February 14, 1955, Wright to the Foreign Office.

81. PRO, FO 371/115751, March 1, 1955, Shuckburgh to Parker.

82. PRO, FO 371/115758, March 11, 1955, Serpell to Rose.

83. PRO, CAB 129/74, C. (55) 70, March 14, 1955.

84. PRO, FO 371/115758, March 21, 1955, minute of meeting of the Working Party on Anglo-Iraqi Negotiations.

85. PRO, FO 371/115760, December 20, 1955, "Exchange of Notes Between the Government of the United Kingdom . . . and the Government of Iraq Referring to the Special Agreement signed at Baghdad on the 4th of April, 1955."

86. Gulshan Dietl, *The Dulles Era: America Enters West Asia* (New Delhi, 1986), 55; Devereaux, *British Defense Policy*, 168–69; Gallman, *Iraq under General Nuri*, 174–76; PRO, PREM 11/1895, May 9, 1957, Caccia to the Foreign Office.

87. Marr, *Modern History of Iraq*, 155–59; Gallman, *Iraq under General Nuri*, 188–96.

Chapter Four

A Threat to Empire: The Buraimi Dispute

Fear of being replaced by the United States in the Middle East was not the only worry London had concerning its empire in that region. Churchill's government also faced a direct challenge to Britain's position in the Persian Gulf from the expansionist designs of the House of Saud. Aside from Egypt, the American-allied Kingdom of Saudi Arabia proved to be the Arab regime that caused the biggest problems for the British in the Middle East. While deeper issues were at play, the formal diplomatic disagreements between the British and the Saudis centered on border disputes involving Riyadh and the British-allied Gulf States. In particular, the struggle for the Buraimi Oasis caused a great deal of international tension. As Saudi Arabia was America's only Arab ally, the dispute over Buraimi provides a valuable perspective on Anglo-American relations and raises interesting questions. How did Washington react to this conflict between its European partner and its Middle Eastern friend? Did Britain still possess the strength to pursue a policy on the Arabian Peninsula that the United States did not support?

The Buraimi dispute began in earnest in August 1952 when a Saudi Arabian official, Turki bin Ataishan, accompanied by a party of forty armed men, seized the disputed oasis from Britain's allies, Abu Dhabi and Muscat. Since 1922, attempts to settle the ill-defined eastern borders of Saudi Arabia had resulted in intermittent negotiations between the Saudis and the British, who acted on behalf of their Persian Gulf allies. In 1949 the Saudis first laid claim to the lush oasis of Buraimi and the surrounding territory which, preliminary investigations suggested, contained oil. In the London Agreement of August 1951 the two parties agreed to halt the prospecting operations of their respective oil companies in the disputed region until the border could be finalized in meetings set to begin the next winter in Damman Saudi Arabia. In 1952 the Damman Conference adjourned without reaching a final settlement.

Before negotiations could resume the Saudis dispatched Turki to occupy the oasis in the name of King Ibn Saud. The British protested the occupation as an infringement of the London Agreement and a violation of territory belonging to Muscat and Abu Dhabi. Seeking to avoid violence, London dissuaded the Sultan of Muscat from taking military action against Turki. In October 1952, Great Britain, acting on behalf of Muscat and Abu Dhabi, signed the Buraimi Standstill Agreement to facilitate further negotiations. The Standstill Agreement, brokered by Raymond Hare, American ambassador to Saudi Arabia, called for both parties to maintain their current positions and refrain from introducing any more troops into the area pending the resumption of negotiations. The agreement forbade all "provocative" activities and attempts to influence the loyalty of the local tribes. In November 1952 the British Foreign Office proposed that the dispute be submitted to arbitration. On January 5, 1953, the British rejected a Saudi counterproposal that the sovereignty of Buraimi be determined by a plebiscite and renewed their call for arbitration. The Truman administration promptly informed the Saudi government that it supported the British arbitration proposal. When Eisenhower took office a short time later, the dispute over Buraimi remained in this unsettled state.[1]

BRITISH AND AMERICAN INTERESTS IN THE GULF

By the 1950s Britain had enjoyed a strong presence in the Persian Gulf for centuries. In the seventeenth century the British East India Company first established a British presence in the Gulf and the Arabian Peninsula. With the expansion of British control over India in the eighteenth century, the importance of the Gulf grew in London's estimation. In the nineteenth and twentieth centuries, London codified its relations with friendly Gulf states in a series of treaties. In 1892 Great Britain agreed to conduct the foreign relations of, and provide defense for, seven small sheikhdoms on the Trucial coast of the Arabian Peninsula, collectively known as the Trucial States. London expanded this protected status to Kuwait in 1914, Qatar in 1935, and Bahrain in 1951. The Sultanate of Muscat and Oman, while not officially a British Protected State, enjoyed a commercial treaty with the United Kingdom as well as London's political guidance and military support.[2]

Britain's original interest in the Persian Gulf arose from a desire to protect the communications route to India. By the 1950s the importance of the Persian Gulf for Britain lay more in its potential for oil production and its strategic position relative to the larger states of the Middle East. As oil treaties fell under the heading of foreign relations, London had the right to approve all oil concessions granted by the Protected States. However, British-owned companies did not exercise a monopoly over oil production in the region. American-owned firms and jointly held Anglo-American companies shared oil production in the British-controlled Gulf.[3]

Unlike Britain's centuries-old ties to the Gulf region, the United States only began to develop commercial links in the area in the 1930s. The American position in the Gulf centered on Saudi Arabia. While the Saudis had once looked to London as their principal ally, by the end of the 1940s American influence came to predominate. King Ibn Saud, despite continuing to receive British financial aid as late as World War II, harbored deep suspicions about the British and their Hashimite allies in Iraq and Jordan. The House of Saud had driven the Hashimite dynasty out of central Arabia in the 1920s to establish the Kingdom of Saudi Arabia, and relations between the two Arab royal families had never recovered. In 1933 the Standard Oil Company of California (Socal) received the oil concession for the Kingdom of Saudi Arabia at a time when few experts believed that Saudi Arabia had any oil. Socal invited other American companies to share the concession and created a jointly owned subsidiary known as the Arabian-American Oil Company (Aramco).

The United States government played no role in either the establishment or development of the Aramco concession. However, after the Second World War the State Department developed a deeper interest in Saudi Arabia as a source of oil for Western Europe and as an anti-Communist ally in the Middle East. After establishing an embassy in Saudi Arabia in 1949, the United States leased an air base at Dhahran from the Saudis. Dhahran quickly became the most valuable American military base in the Middle East. In 1950, to promote stability and modernization in its new ally, the State Department encouraged Aramco to provide 50 percent of the profits from the exploitation of Saudi oil to the Saudi government. This more equitable revenue sharing plan significantly decreased the chances that Riyadh would nationalize Aramco's holdings. In addition to the oil contract and the Dhahran air base, the Kingdom of Saudi Arabia was also tied to the United States by economic and military aid, making it Washington's closest friend in the Arab world.[4]

British and American interests clearly ran at cross-purposes in the Anglo-Saudi dispute over Buraimi. To the British, protection of their Gulf allies was vital to the defense of their empire. British prestige in the Middle East would suffer a great blow if they could not maintain the territory of their oldest allies in the region. The value of Persian Gulf oil added a concrete economic dimension to London's desire to resist Saudi claims to Buraimi. Washington faced a more ambiguous situation. For the United States, Saudi Arabia represented not a threat but a valuable ally in an unstable part of the world. Of course Washington was also keenly aware of the importance of the British in maintaining stability in the region as well as the value of the Anglo-American alliance in the wider struggle against Communism. Trying to bridge the gap between the British and the Saudis, the Truman administration had facilitated the Standstill Agreement to allow for a peaceful settlement of the dispute. However, the Buraimi quarrel was not quickly resolved, and the Eisenhower administration found itself under pressure from both London and Riyadh to back their respective positions.

EISENHOWER TAKES OFFICE

In the first week of 1953, shortly before Dwight Eisenhower's inauguration, the British Foreign Office formally outlined its views on the Buraimi dispute. Whitehall charged that the Saudis had continually disregarded the Standstill Agreement by bribing and intimidating the tribes of the Buraimi area away from their "traditional allegiance" to the Sultan of Muscat and the Sheikh of Abu Dhabi. London stood by its offer for arbitration, rejecting the Saudi call for a plebiscite to be overseen by a tripartite commission composed of American, British, and Saudi members. The British believed that any plebiscite would be heavily influenced in favor of Riyadh due to Saudi bribery of the local tribes. Fearing that Saudi Arabia would press even more expansive claims against the territories of its Gulf allies if it did not stand firm at Buraimi, London decided to dispatch armored cars, RAF jets, and warships to the Trucial States. Whitehall also expanded the locally recruited, British-led forces known as the Trucial Oman Levies. In a message sent to all diplomatic missions, the Foreign Office stressed the importance of maintaining the British alliances in the Persian Gulf. According to the cable, the "discovery of oil and the importance of the Persian Gulf in worldwide communications has greatly increased the value of this relationship not only to ourselves but to the whole Western world." The Foreign Office went on to point out that Britain's policy arose not just from a desire for oil but also from a duty to protect the rights of its allies. In contrast, London charged the Saudis with pressing their claim to Buraimi only after the discovery of oil near the oasis. The Foreign Office dismissed any suggestion that the dispute "represented a struggle between American and British oil interests," explaining that American firms owned 24 percent of the British company that held the oil concession in the Trucial States.[5]

With the dispatch of the military reinforcements to the Trucial States, code-named Operation Boxer, London hoped to achieve a greater degree of flexibility in the dispute. London ordered the commanders of the augmented British forces to repel any further Saudi incursions into undisputed territory and to maintain the status quo in the disputed zone but to use "the greatest restraint" in carrying out their duties.[6] On a more aggressive note the British Chiefs of Staff foresaw the use of these forces to impose a unilaterally declared frontier if the Saudi government rejected arbitration.[7]

The newly elected Eisenhower administration found itself besieged by requests for support from both sides of the dispute. Ambassador Raymond Hare and the State Department received complaints from Saudi officials that the British had violated the Standstill Agreement by intimidating and bribing the local tribes. According to Ambassador Hare, the Saudis were angry at what they perceived as American support for London.[8]

In early 1953, Saudi Foreign Minister Prince Faisal paid an extended visit to Washington. In a March 2 meeting with Secretary of State Dulles the Saudi foreign minister outlined his agenda. Faisal wanted the Eisenhower administration to honor an October 1950 pledge made by the Truman administration to protect Saudi territorial integrity. The prince also complained about the paucity of American military and economic aid to Riyadh. Lastly, Faisal turned to the Buraimi dispute. He decried what he described as the hostility of Britain, a nation he characterized as having once been a close friend to Saudi Arabia. The prince asked for American backing for the Saudi proposal of a plebiscite for Buraimi. Dulles promised that he would look into the matters of the Truman letter and American aid. As for Buraimi, the secretary admitted that he did not have full information on the dispute but he currently supported the British proposal for arbitration. Dulles described arbitration as the internationally accepted "best means of settling such matters" and pointed to America's use of arbitration in border disputes with Canada and Mexico. Faisal replied that arbitration might be acceptable for the Arabian frontier disputes in general but not in the specific case of Buraimi, which clearly lay within the realm of Ibn Saud.[9] When Eisenhower met with Faisal later in the day, the president made no mention of the frontier issue but expressed hope that American relations with the Arabs would grow in "confidence and trust" so that together they could meet the threat of the "godless materialist forces of communism."[10]

Two weeks later, Under Secretary of State Walter Bedell Smith informed the Saudi ambassador of the official American response to Faisal's inquiries. The Eisenhower administration "emphatically" reaffirmed President Truman's "interest in the territorial integrity and independence of Saudi Arabia." President Eisenhower also approved a grant of military aid to the Saudis. On the issue of Buraimi, however, the United States felt compelled to continue to support arbitration as the best means of settlement. In order to promote this plan, Bedell Smith suggested that any arbitration would include a "consultation of the wishes of the inhabitants and could thus embrace to some extent the [Saudi] plebiscite idea." The Saudi ambassador, Sheikh Asad Al Faqih, expressed appreciation for the military aid and the reaffirmation of the Truman letter but said that King Ibn Saud would be unhappy over the arbitration proposal. The ambassador proposed that the United States agree to be part of an independent investigation team charged with looking into alleged breaches of the Standstill Agreement. The sheikh suggested that American participation in such an investigation might prompt King Ibn Saud to accept arbitration. While not rejecting this idea out of hand, Bedell Smith would not commit the United States to any investigation.[11]

Despite this initial rebuff the Saudis continued to apply pressure in Washington. In a March 23, 1953, meeting with Dulles, Prince Faisal expressed King Ibn Saud's displeasure with Washington. According to Faisal, the king "felt that the unusually close ties between the United States and Saudi Arabia called for more active US intervention in the Buraimi dispute in such a way as to protect and advance Saudi interests." The prince concluded by saying that he "did not feel he could return to his father [the King] without evidence of greater goodwill" on the part of the United States. Dulles promised to reconsider the matter.[12]

However, the American position on arbitration could not be so easily reversed by the Saudis. In a memo to Dulles, Henry Byroade, assistant secretary of state for Near Eastern, South Asian, and African affairs, urged that the United States maintain its support for arbitration. Byroade's analysis pointed to the weakness of the Saudi claim to undisputed sovereignty over Buraimi and their charges of British aggression. Byroade agreed with the British that Turki's bribery and intimidation in Buraimi would make the proposed plebiscite invalid. According to Byroade, impartial arbitration held the best hopes for a fair settlement. Arbitration had the added virtue of not directly involving the United States in settling the dispute.[13]

Dulles agreed with Byroade, and Bedell Smith passed along the State Department's decision to continue to support arbitration to Prince Faisal a few days later. In order to soften the blow, Bedell Smith assured the skeptical Saudi foreign minister that Anthony Eden and Sir Roger Makins had pledged to the United States that Britain had not, and would not, violate the Standstill Agreement. Speaking off the record, Bedell Smith told Faisal that the United States wanted to avoid pressing the Churchill government too firmly on this matter, as the Tory government might collapse if faced with a foreign policy defeat at Buraimi. Faisal caustically asked "whether this meant that Britain had to rule the world as it had been doing in the past or the cabinet would fall." Bedell Smith responded by saying that Anglo-American relations were currently strained and London already believed that Washington favored the Saudis in the dispute. This made it impossible for the American government to "put pressure on the United Kingdom." The under secretary implored the prince to appreciate the delicate position that the United States found itself in as a result of the dispute.[14]

Officials at the State Department's Near Eastern desk remained unconcerned about the Saudi reaction to America's continued support for arbitration. Despite the disappointment expressed by Prince Faisal, the State Department believed that his ill temper represented more bluster than genuine anger. The State Department dismissed King Ibn Saud's hopes for direct action by the United States as arising from his senility. The department believed that "it is not too much to suppose that Prince Faisal never seriously entertained such hopes" and that his request could be explained by "the common practice of Arabs to ask for more than they expect to gain." State Department officials argued that the Saudis should be happy with what they had been promised by the administration. In fact, the State Department believed that the Arab world in general had high hopes of better relations with the United States now that Eisenhower occupied the White House.[15]

Although Washington would not agree to support the Saudi position on Buraimi, it hoped that the decision to grant military aid to Riyadh would help maintain good Saudi-American relations. In arguing in favor of giving aid to Saudi Arabia, the State Department reminded the Department of Defense of the strategic importance of the Dhahran air base. The agreement on the Dhahran air base, signed on June 18, 1951, would be liable for modification or cancellation in June 1956. If the United States hoped to expand the facilities at the base, good relations with Riyadh needed to be maintained.[16]

At the time of Faisal's visit to Washington, Foreign Secretary Eden also paid a call to the American capital. Dulles and Bedell Smith informed Eden that the Saudis were placing "strong pressure" on the United States to support them on the Buraimi dispute. As Ibn Saud seemed dead set against agreeing to arbitration, Bedell Smith suggested that the British "find some other term" to describe the process, possibly some Arabic equivalent. Eden stood by his government's offer for arbitration, which he described as inherently fair, and hinted that London might increase pressure on Riyadh by cutting off the Saudis in Buraimi from supply. The foreign secretary claimed that this action would not break the Standstill Agreement. Summarizing Washington's attitude, Eden reported to Churchill, "while the Americans were supporting us loyally in our demand for arbitration, they were acutely embarrassed by the Saudi attitude and by the pressure which Ibn Saud is clearly exercising upon them by the threat to their oil supplies." Eden expressed to the prime minister the hope that the United States and Britain would "make a supreme effort to reach understanding on all the Middle East problems which were in danger of wrecking Anglo-American understanding throughout this area."[17]

Prime Minister Churchill pronounced the American attitude on the Buraimi dispute as "satisfactory," although he characterized the suggestion to make the arbitration offer more amenable to the Saudis as "slightly sinister." Churchill saw no reason to back down from the Saudis, as reports indicated that the local tribes were moving back to support of the British-backed rulers.[18] G. C. Pelham, British ambassador to Saudi Arabia, supported this hard line, suggesting that the Saudis hoped that, as long as they resisted compromise, they could achieve their objective by swaying American and world opinion against Britain. The ambassador believed that charges of imperialism were sure to be leveled at London by the Saudis if the dispute continued without an agreeable solution.[19]

With the Eisenhower administration in office, the Churchill government seemed to believe that the time for compromise with the Saudis had passed. Truman's administration had pressured the British to accept the Standstill Agreement that left the Saudis in position in Buraimi, but Eisenhower had now replaced Truman. Perhaps Eden and Churchill believed that their old friend "Ike" would offer more support for their position. By early 1953 the British were unwilling to make even cosmetic changes in their offer for arbitration. Eden had even brought up the possibility of using force to blockade Turki bin Ataishan and his troops in Buraimi. The Saudis also apparently hoped that the change in American governments offered them an opportunity to advance their case in Washington. The United States had been placed in the uncomfortable position of trying to placate the equally inflexible Saudis and British. Despite concerns about the continuing availability of the Dhahran air base, Washington continued to support arbitration. This position would place a severe strain on American relations with the Kingdom of Saudi Arabia, while Britain expressed little or no appreciation to Washington.

THE BRITISH BLOCKADE OF BURAIMI

Eden's threat in Washington to use force to blockade Buraimi became a reality in the spring of 1953. On March 16, 1953, Eden presented a memo to the British Cabinet that outlined plans for a more forceful response to the Buraimi dispute. Eden argued that Britain's repeated offers of arbitration had failed to move the Saudis closer to compromise. Instead, Turki continued to try to induce the tribes to accept Saudi sovereignty. Now that Operation Boxer had provided the British with local military superiority around the oasis, Eden wanted to use force to curtail the suborning activities of Turki. Eden noted "our friends (and enemies) in the Gulf are watching critically the outcome of this trial of strength between us and the Saudis." The foreign secretary suggested that Britain should renounce the London Agreement and the Standstill Agreement and effect a blockade of Turki in Buraimi while renewing calls for arbitration. Eden predicted that Riyadh would react sharply but would not resist with military force. The most damaging move the Saudis might take would be to bring the dispute to the United Nations, where widespread anticolonial sentiment would be focused on the British position in the Gulf. As for the American reaction, Eden believed that the "Saudis expect and demand assistance from the US in international disputes and are seldom disappointed." However, Eden believed that as the United States had so far backed the British call for arbitration, they deserved to be forewarned about London's military plans. Eden hoped that American acquiescence could be obtained, but he pointedly wrote, "I do not imagine that they would . . . approve, nor indeed would their approval be sought."[20]

Eden determined that the Saudis would only be officially informed of the blockade on the day it began. On the other hand, the United States would be given two days' notice. British Ambassador Sir Roger Makins received instructions from Eden to "break the news if possible to Mr. Dulles personally" and make it clear that the blockade "is not British 'imperialism' vs. Saudi 'nationalism' but Saudi 'imperialism' attempting to override the rights and interests of lesser Arab rulers who are under our protection or are friendly to us."[21] With Dulles unavailable, Makins presented the information to Henry Byroade on March 31, 1953. Makins noted that the assistant secretary "received the news gloomily." Byroade believed that the Saudis were sure to take the matter to the UN and attempt to invoke Truman's October 1950 promise of American support for Saudi territorial integrity. The British Embassy suggested that the best method of countering any Saudi diplomatic pressure would be for the United States to publicly acknowledge that Riyadh had initiated the aggression at Buraimi. This suggestion failed to impress Byroade. According to Makins, Byroade "seemed to think that Saudi expansion into the coastal territories was sooner or later inevitable, and that Her Majesty's Government were consequently swimming against the tide."[22]

Meanwhile, in London, Permanent Under Secretary of State for Foreign Affairs Sir William Strang asked American Ambassador Winthrop Aldrich for continued American pressure on the Saudis to accept arbitration. When Strang confronted Aldrich with Byroade's alleged comments about the inevitability of Saudi expansion into the Gulf coast, the ambassador denied that this statement reflected official American policy.[23] It seems likely that Byroade's comments arose from his anger that the British, despite Washington's backing of arbitration, had decided to use force, rather than from a conviction that the Saudis would end up with Buraimi.

In spite of any anger at London's decision to blockade the oasis, Washington reacted as favorably as Whitehall could have hoped. When the British announced the blockade of Turki on April 2, 1953, Dulles cabled Ambassador Hare in Jidda with his instructions. If the Saudis asked for American assistance on the strength of the Truman letter, Dulles told Hare to inform the

Saudis that the letter was never meant "to serve as a cloak for Saudi expeditions into disputed territory." If Washington had been consulted before the dispatch of Turki to Buraimi, Dulles added, the Saudis would have been advised against such action, as the area is clearly not uncontested Saudi territory. As for the Saudi plan to settle the dispute by plebiscite, the United States did "not intend becoming associated with Saudi practice of sending governors into disputed areas on [the] basis [of] alleged popular demand and having their position established by plebiscite which would undoubtedly be contested." The State Department wanted Hare to continue to urge the Saudis to accept arbitration or another alternative to a plebiscite.[24]

London was pleased with the American reaction to the announcement of the blockade. The Foreign Office concluded that "on the whole it may be said that a satisfactory impression of Anglo-American solidarity in the Saudi Arabian frontier dispute has been created in the minds of the Saudi Arabian Government by the present administration, even though their support for arbitration should not be interpreted by HMG as a sign of complete approval of our policy." London hoped that the United States "would continue to recommend arbitration to the Saudi Arabian Government."[25]

The Churchill government's decision to employ military forces to put pressure on the Saudis was clearly an aggressive step that the Americans would have advised against if consulted beforehand. Great Britain's independence of thought and action was demonstrated by the fact that London only gave Washington two days' notice of the move and never intended to discuss the advisability of the plan with the Americans. Washington must have realized that the Saudis would be angered by the British blockade. Surprisingly, instead of offering at least a show of sympathy to Riyadh, Dulles's response was to lecture the Saudis about the aggressive nature of Turki's original occupation of the oasis. London could not realistically have expected more backing from the United States. Although the British were moderately grateful for Washington's placid acceptance of the blockade, they still complained that the Americans did not fully support them at Buraimi. The British attitude shows little concern for American interests, as any more support from Washington would almost certainly have led to a dramatic decline in Saudi-American relations.

OIL BECOMES AN ISSUE

Once the British renounced the London and the Standstill Agreements, the issue of oil in the disputed zone became more prominent. Even before the British blockade of Turki began, the Foreign Office informed the Iraqi Petroleum Company (IPC) that its operations in the disputed zone could resume shortly once the legal constraints of the London Agreement of 1951 were removed. That agreement had barred all oil companies from the disputed area. On April 2, 1953, when IPC declared that it "was most anxious to get to work in the area from which they had previously been excluded," the Foreign Office encouraged it to resume the search for oil.[26]

In Washington, the State Department invited Aramco to consult on the Buraimi dispute. On April 3, 1953, State Department officials met with Aramco executives and Mr. Young, an American legal consultant to the Saudi government. According to Young, "Aramco had no present intentions to seek oil in Buraimi, or any other disputed area." In fact, Young claimed that Aramco had informed the Saudi government that it would renounce its corporate oil concession in any "disputed territories" if it would help to settle any border disputes. Young expressed the hope that if Aramco renounced its concession, London would be convinced that neither the company nor the Saudis were motivated by greed for oil and a compromise could be quickly reached. Deputy Assistant Secretary of State John Jernegan told the oilmen that he believed that even if oil were not part of the picture, "the British would act as they have purely out of their prestige considerations."[27]

Aramco executives were also involved in diplomacy in London. In April 1953, Aramco officials met with British and American diplomats at the Foreign Office. Aramco Vice President Terry Duce, fresh from his talks with the State Department, met with Archibald Ross, head of the Eastern Department of the Foreign Office, as well as executives of the American oil companies that controlled a portion of the Iraqi Petroleum Company. According to Ross, "Mr. Duce's object was to convince me that his company was not behind the recent Saudi claims or in any way responsible for the dispatch of Turki to Buraimi. His company were entirely ready to relinquish their concession in respect to the disputed areas. They were, however, no more than the servant of the concessionary Government, and they had to mind their step." Duce expressed the opinion that all the oil companies should stay out of the dispute and simply hope that the two governments would come to a quick agreement. Ross suggested that the best way to assure a quick settlement would be for Aramco to support arbitration as a fair solution to the problem.[28]

The American Embassy's report to the State Department of the aforementioned meeting contained an analysis of British motivation in the Buraimi dispute that downplayed the importance of oil. The embassy concluded that, while the desire to protect oil interests and a "genuine feeling of responsibility towards the interests of the Sheiks" played a role in London's calculations, the overriding concern probably centered on "prestige considerations." The report went on to state, "There is widespread concern in this country, particularly among the Conservatives, about the loss of British prestige as a result of events in Iran and Egypt. . . . Under these circumstances [it is] . . . extremely doubtful that the present government in any event would, in the foreseeable future, be willing or even find it possible to make large-scale concessions to the Saudis in the Persian Gulf."[29]

The question of oil in the disputed territories was one that grew in intensity as the Buraimi quarrel continued. At this stage in the dispute the British and American oil companies seemed willing to cooperate, but later events would find Aramco in a dangerous showdown with London.

THE PUSH FOR ARBITRATION

By late April 1953, after Buraimi had been blockaded for weeks, Saudi Arabia appeared ready to compromise on the arbitration issue. On April 19 King Ibn Saud informed British Ambassador Pelham that he would consider the principle of neutral arbitration as a fair means of resolving the border disputes on his eastern frontier. The Saudi conditions for arbitration included taking the opinions of the local tribes into consideration, withdrawal of all forces introduced into the area since the signing of the Standstill Agreement in October 1952, and a resumption of the London and Standstill Agreements. Pelham urged London to accept these terms, even though it meant leaving Turki in Buraimi and having IPC stop oil prospecting in the disputed zone. The ambassador believed that Saudi Arabia had made an important concession by offering these terms.[30]

In London, Churchill, who was acting as foreign secretary while Eden made a lengthy recovery from surgery, resisted the idea of any compromise with the Saudis. Sir William Strang suggested to Churchill that London propose that instead of the withdrawal of the British troops, a neutral supervisory commission be established to ensure that neither side's forces took any actions that would influence the outcome of arbitration.[31] Churchill belligerently replied, "It was decided that if we did not get arbitration we should use force." The prime minister said he never would have proposed continuing negotiations with the Saudis after the blockade began if he "thought that a policy of concessions was to follow from it."[32] Adamant against the idea of neutral observation, which he characterized as "meddling by foreigners," Churchill sent a message to Ibn Saud suggesting that "it shall be a matter of honor between us that no advantages are to be taken by either side in the military position" and that Turki be allowed to remain in Buraimi pending the arbitration settlement.[33] Ibn Saud refused Churchill's proposal, claiming that the present military situation gave the advantage to the British. According to the king, the status quo of October 1952, before Operation Boxer increased

British forces and Turki had been isolated, had to be restored. The Saudis believed that a commission appointed by a neutral arbitration body, not a sense of honor, would be the best method of overseeing the disputed area until a final solution appeared.[34]

Minister of State Selwyn Lloyd suggested to Churchill that an acceptable compromise would be a mutual withdrawal of Turki and all British-controlled forces from the disputed area until a final accord was reached. Lloyd believed that this proposal would "put us in a very strong position in the eyes of world opinion [and] should command useful support from the United States."[35] Churchill replied that any compromise would be bad for the empire as a whole. Churchill claimed that Britain suffered "all this encroachment and ill treatment in many parts of the world because it is felt that you have only to kick the British or push them and they will clear out. This impression grew up from the Abadan scuttle and has cost us a lot ever since."[36] Lloyd countered that the Foreign Office as a whole supported the idea of mutual withdrawal as an acceptable compromise. The minister of state argued that if Churchill blocked a compromise, London would lose the chance for arbitration, Turki would still be in Buraimi causing trouble, and the United States would probably withdraw the support that it had so far given to Britain.[37]

Under this pressure from his own Foreign Office, and perhaps fearing that continued refusal to bend to an American-supported compromise might harm his own ongoing efforts to cajole Eisenhower into an East-West summit, Churchill finally agreed to propose mutual withdrawal to the Saudis. On June 2, 1953, Ambassador Pelham received instructions to make this new offer to Riyadh. The cable added that London hoped that it would not have to stop British oil companies from operating in the disputed zone, although the final settlement of the arbitration commission would determine the fate of the oil concessions.[38] When presented with the British offer the Saudis balked at the idea of mutual withdrawal, pointing out that Turki and his men would have to retire seven hundred kilometers to the nearest undisputed Saudi town while the British-led forces would only have to retreat fifty kilometers to the Trucial Coast.[39] Apparently, the Saudis did not believe that admitting this disparity hindered their claim to Buraimi at all.

While London and Riyadh were haggling over the terms of arbitration, Secretary of State Dulles paid a visit to Saudi Arabia in May 1953. In a brief meeting with Dulles on May 18, King Ibn Saud expressed his profound displeasure with American policy.[40] In a more detailed meeting involving Crown Prince Saud, Foreign Minister Prince Faisal, and Deputy Foreign Minister Sheikh Yussef, the Saudis repeated their belief that the United States had let Riyadh down and failed to live up to Truman's commitment of October 1950. The crown prince warned that if the United States proved not to be a loyal friend, then "Saudi Arabia would have to find some other way to maintain her interests." The crown prince claimed that the United Kingdom had repaid the Saudi offer to accept arbitration by continuing to use force in Buraimi. Dulles refuted Prince Saud's charges. He denied that the British were using force at Buraimi. The secretary said that the Truman letter did not cover the Buraimi dispute because the Saudis did not have an undisputed claim to the oasis. Additionally, the letter only promised American concern for Saudi territorial integrity; it did not offer a firm guarantee. Dulles protested that the United States had been trying to put pressure on the British on Saudi Arabia's behalf, but that Washington could not force London to agree with its advice. Dulles pointedly asked Saud if he believed that the United States should go to war against Britain over the Buraimi dispute. Dulles again urged that Saudi Arabia agree to settle the frontier by arbitration. In an attempt to somewhat mollify the angry Saudis, Dulles urged them not to give up on the possibility of the United States convincing London to agree to a reasonable solution. However, Dulles said that he could not discuss any details of the American diplomatic activities, as he did not want to publicly embarrass the Churchill government.[41] The next day, in a less contentious meeting, Prince Faisal asked Dulles to urge the British to accept the Saudi arbitration proposal of a return to the Standstill Agreement and the equalization of forces in the region until the final settlement.[42] Although he did not admit it to the Saudis, after the trip, Dulles privately noted that while Britain had a sound legal position, the shift of the Buraimi area tribes' allegiance to the Saudis seemed "natural and must be taken into account."[43]

Ambassador Hare considered the result of Dulles's trip a mixed blessing. On the positive side Dulles had impressed Ibn Saud and calmed the crown prince, who now had high hopes for American assistance in settling the dispute. On the other hand, Foreign Minister Prince Faisal had adopted a very negative attitude toward America and spoke in favor of Saudi Arabia adopting a neutral stance in the Cold War.[44] While Hare saw some good coming from Dulles's trip, some State Department officials feared that the Saudi-American relationship had been badly damaged. In particular, Henry Byroade believed that King Ibn Saud might end the Aramco concession and expel the United States from the Dhahran air base due to lack of American support.[45]

As American concerns over relations with Saudi Arabia were growing, London seemed immune to Washington's calls for even modest steps toward conciliation. On May 22, 1953, Churchill refused the State Department's suggestion that the withdrawal of some of the British troops in the Buraimi region might be helpful in calming the agitated King Ibn Saud.[46] Off the record, the prime minister told Ambassador Aldrich that "he really thought he knew more about Ibn Saud than Dulles did and that it was slightly irritating that

Dulles, in his globe-trotting progress, should take pains at every point to sympathize with those who were trying to kick out or do down the British."[47]

Despite evoking ire from both parties in the dispute, Washington continued to push for a peaceful settlement. In June, when Churchill eventually made his offer to the Saudis of mutual withdrawal from Buraimi, the State Department instructed Ambassador Hare to urge Riyadh to accept. The Saudis made a counterproposal for arbitration terms: the United Kingdom to end the blockade of Turki, the equalization of forces in the area, and the end to all provocation at Buraimi with the arbitration body to be given the power to judge violations of the new agreement. On June 19, 1953, Washington urged London and Riyadh to come to a compromise based on what it saw as a reasonable offer by the Saudis.[48] However, London rejected the Saudi offer, claiming that the local tribes would see an equalization of forces with Turki still in place as a total victory for the Saudis. The Foreign Office remained intransigent despite acknowledging that the United States hoped a settlement would placate the Saudis and protect the Aramco concession and the Dhahran air base.[49]

The State Department's frustration with Britain grew as a result of London's failure to compromise. In a letter to Dulles, Assistant Secretary of State Byroade placed the blame on the British for failing to settle the dispute. According to Byroade, the Near Eastern Affairs Bureau held the opinion that the "British attitude toward [the] Saudi proposals . . . has been unnecessarily inflexible and we believe that they might make some concession in order to get the process of arbitration started." He suggested that Dulles press London to make the necessary concessions.[50] Dulles would get his chance when Acting Foreign Secretary Lord Salisbury visited Washington in July 1953.

At a meeting with Salisbury on July 11, 1953, the secretary of state jokingly said, "We appear to be allied to the opposing forces." The dispute at Buraimi was no joke, however, and both sides claimed to be under great pressure from their respective Arab friends. After a review of the current state of negotiations, Henry Byroade proposed a new compromise to Salisbury. Arbitration would begin with the current forces in place, but the blockade on Turki would be lifted if the Saudis stopped their suborning activities. To insure that the agreement would not be breached, an observation commission made up of one Saudi, one British, and one neutral observer would be established. Bedell Smith added that, while the British may believe that the Saudis had agreed to the principle of arbitration because of their military measures, in fact, Riyadh had been influenced more by the many hours that the State Department had spent pushing the idea of arbitration.[51] The British Cabinet, with both Eden and Churchill absent due to illness, found the American proposal unacceptable. Allowing Turki to remain would cause too much harm to British prestige in the Gulf. The Cabinet concluded that the "potential value of the oil concessions [in the Gulf] made it specially important that we should retain our influence there."[52]

At the next meeting between Dulles and Salisbury, the marquess outlined the Cabinet's objections to the American plan and urged that Eisenhower personally endorse mutual withdrawal to Ibn Saud. Dulles replied that the United States had pushed the Saudis as far as they were likely to go. Washington placed great value on good relations with Saudi Arabia because of Dhahran and the Aramco concession and did not want to further strain the friendship. Under pressure from the secretary of state, Salisbury agreed to discuss the matter again with London.[53]

Despite American pleas to be reasonable, the Foreign Office held the opinion that Britain should not compromise. London believed that American concerns about the possible damage to Western relations with Saudi Arabia were misplaced. The Saudis, if unchecked, would continue to make expansionist claims against their Arab neighbors. According to the Foreign Office, if the United States succeeded "in getting us to knuckle under to Ibn Saud the effect immediately and in the long run . . . will be far more damaging to them and to our joint interests than the temporary embarrassment of standing up to the Saudis."[54] Salisbury placed this argument before the Cabinet, which concurred that there should be no compromise on the issue of Turki remaining in Buraimi.[55] Lord Salisbury made the British position clear in a letter to Dulles delivered on July 28, 1953. Any compromise that could be seen as a Saudi victory would undermine Britain's, and also America's, relations with the other oil-rich states in the Persian Gulf. If the United States did not feel that it could influence Riyadh to accept mutual withdrawal, than the blockade would have to remain in place.[56]

On August 28, 1953, Dulles replied to Salisbury that the British stance disappointed the United States. Dulles pointed out that Washington had loyally stood by the United Kingdom in support of arbitration. He complained,

> Perhaps you are not aware . . . of the strain which our support imposed upon our friendly relationship with King Ibn Saud. I am sure that you will agree that Saudi Arabia is assuming an increasingly important position in the pattern of our common defense. While recognizing the importance of your position in the Persian Gulf, I feel strongly that in the days ahead of us it will be of paramount importance to both of us to have the friendship and confidence of the ruler of Saudi Arabia."[57]

While the Americans and British argued over the value of a compromise with the Saudis on Buraimi, Riyadh took an important step toward a peaceful settlement of the dispute. On September 24, 1953, the Saudi ambassador to London, Sheikh Hafiz Wahba, seemingly broke the impasse at Buraimi with a new proposal that accepted mutual withdrawal if both sides could then introduce a small detachment for policing the oasis while arbitration went forward.[58] On October 13, 1953, Anthony Eden, who had since returned to the Foreign Office, informed Dulles of the Saudi offer and the fact that negotiations were now under way with the Saudi government to confirm London's acceptance of the proposal.[59] While Eden's message to Dulles expressed cautious optimism about the negotiations, he was less moderate with his Foreign Office colleagues. On his first day back he complained to his private secretary, Evelyn Shuckburgh, that Turki should have been violently removed from Buraimi already. If the Saudis dragged their feet on Ambassador Wahba's new proposal, Eden wanted to kidnap Turki. Foreign Office officials persuaded Eden against this course of action, as Britain still needed American cooperation in Egypt and Iran.[60]

Although calmer heads dissuaded Eden from an attempted kidnapping, London had made very few compromises over Buraimi since Eisenhower came into office. Britain would not succumb to American pressure to compromise, even when Dulles explained how important Washington believed Saudi Arabian friendship was to the overall Western position in the Middle East. As far as Whitehall was concerned, American Cold War considerations took a back seat to Britain's imperial interests in the Persian Gulf.

THE OIL ISSUE MOVES TO THE FOREFRONT

The vexing question of oil appeared during Anglo-Saudi negotiations of Ambassador Wahba's proposal. As early as May 1953, in order to facilitate an agreement, the Saudi government had intimated to London that it might be willing to grant British companies an oil concession in any areas that were awarded to the Saudis by arbitration. Riyadh claimed that Aramco, which already had plenty of oil-producing areas, could be made to accept this arrangement.[61] By September this offer held increased interest to London as the British oil prospectors now operating in the disputed zone had reported very encouraging results. The Foreign Office noted that the Buraimi dispute, "which had never been confined only to prestige and desert oases" now had another important component.[62] In Eden's opinion the discovery of oil in the disputed area did not have to be seen as a further problem but might help to settle the situation by giving American firms more of an incentive to support an agreement. In a Cabinet meeting, the foreign secretary expressed his belief that any new oil discovered should be exploited by a consortium of American and British companies. As it stood, IPC already had significant American ownership. Eden stated that Anglo-American cooperation on oil production would be helpful not only at Buraimi but "in each of the oil-producing countries of the Middle East."[63]

During the negotiations in the fall of 1953, the main sticking points for the Saudis did not, however, involve oil considerations. In order to begin final arbitration the Saudi government demanded that Britain withdraw from thirteen Trucial Levy posts that Riyadh claimed had been established in disputed territory. In addition, Riyadh demanded that arbitration should only apply to the immediate Buraimi area, not the whole disputed eastern frontier.[64]

Not until February 1954 did London settle on a counterproposal to be presented to King Saud, the heir to King Ibn Saud who had died in November 1953. Initially London had considered requiring that the Saudis follow through on their offer to give British oil companies the concession in any territory awarded to Riyadh. However, upon further consideration, the Foreign Office reduced this demand to a request for Riyadh to consider transfer of the concession to British firms, but only if Aramco agreed. The decision was revised due to both economic and diplomatic considerations. The Iraqi Petroleum Company had urged the Foreign Office not to demand a concession transfer as part of an arbitration agreement. IPC protested that a clash with Aramco might hurt its overall position in the Gulf by causing bad feelings among the American oil companies. Politically, Whitehall believed it would be best not to strain relations with Washington by appearing to be interested primarily in Buraimi's potential oil reserves.

In addition to the issue of oil concessions, London's formal response to the Saudis raised some other questions. London would agree to remove only five of the disputed Levy posts, and it still wished for arbitration to cover a wider area than just the oasis. The final condition laid down by London called for the continued operation of IPC and the Anglo-Iranian Oil Company (AIOC) in the disputed area until final arbitration, at which time the British oil companies would withdraw from any Saudi territory with which Riyadh and Aramco were unwilling to part.[65] When the British government informed Washington of its reply, it made it clear to the United States that the idea of a British oil concession in Saudi territory had originated from the Saudis. London promised not to press the matter if Aramco disapproved.[66] Initially, the State Department reacted favorably to the British proposals and urged the Saudis to accept.[67] However, the oil question soon complicated matters.

Riyadh had never cleared their proposal to have Aramco give up concessionary rights to a British firm with the American oilmen. Contrary to Aramco's claims to the State Department that it was willing to give up concessions in the disputed zone, when King Saud questioned company executives, they rejected the possibility of surrendering any claims in Saudi territory. Rapidly switching directions, the king next asked if Aramco would be willing to undertake exploration in the disputed zone if the Saudi government requested such action. On this point Aramco agreed to cooperate, although the company stipulated that any expedition would take some time to organize.[68]

Although the Foreign Office had specifically rejected the idea of a direct link between a concession transfer and arbitration, Aramco reported to the State Department that the Saudi government believed that Britain would not agree to arbitration unless British companies received concessions in any area awarded to Riyadh. George Wadsworth, the new American ambassador to Saudi Arabia, assured Aramco that the United States supported the British arbitration proposal as a whole but not "any British (IPC) pretension to an oil concession in the disputed area."[69]

It is unclear as to how the disagreement about the transfer of the oil concessions arose. It seems plausible that the Saudi government misrepresented the British request for an oil concession as a demand in order to make the British look bad in Washington. It is also unclear as to why Aramco once told the State Department that it was willing to abandon its concession rights in disputed territory, and then later refused a Saudi request to do just that. One possibility is lack of communication among top Aramco officials. Another possibility is that Aramco and the Saudi government conspired in order to make the British concern for Buraimi seem to arise from a desire to expand their oil holdings at the expense of Aramco.

Whatever the real motivation, Aramco protested to the State Department about the possible transfer of concessions. In a March 10, 1954, meeting in Washington, George Ray, general counsel of Aramco, complained to Assistant Secretary of State Henry Byroade that the company had never been consulted on the issue of oil concessions in the disputed zone. Ray expressed surprise when Byroade explained to him that Aramco Vice President Terry Duce had told the British in April 1953 that Aramco was willing to surrender the concession in the disputed zone if this would help in the formulation of a settlement. Ray explained that the company had no intention of giving up any claim in Saudi Arabia and believed that IPC should be stopped from further operations in the disputed zone, as it would be loath to give up those areas, if necessary, after arbitration. The State Department proved unsympathetic to Aramco during this meeting. Byroade asked Ray why Aramco needed any more oil wells given the vast reserves in undisputed Saudi territory. When Ray described IPC as acting aggressively, a State Department official reminded him that Aramco had been guilty in the past of incursions into British-controlled territory.[70] Dulles attempted to reassure both Aramco and the Saudis that the British proposal for a possible surrender of oil concessions did not constitute a demand and that Riyadh should continue to pursue arbitration based on London's February 1954 plan.[71]

In spite of Dulles's urging, the Saudi government, supported by Aramco, announced that arbitration could only begin if the British oil companies suspended operations in the disputed zone.[72] When Aramco Chairman of the Board William Davies met with Henry Byroade on March 23, 1954, he requested that the State Department support the Aramco/Saudi position on arbitration. After again questioning the need for Aramco to hold onto the oil concession in the disputed zone, Byroade reminded Davies that the United States, above all else, wanted a quick settlement. The State Department planned to suggest a compromise in which both Aramco and IPC would operate in the disputed zone until arbitration was settled. Despite his disapproval of the company's stance, Byroade also assured Davies that the State Department would "do everything it properly can to protect Aramco's interests."[73]

On April 14, 1954, Deputy Assistant Secretary of State John Jernegan informed the British Embassy that the State Department wanted London to exclude any mention of oil and transfer of concessions from its arbitration proposal. He said that both the Saudis and Aramco labored under the false perception that London demanded a surrender of oil concessions as a condition of arbitration. Jernegan warned the embassy that if IPC continued to explore in the disputed zone, then Aramco might be forced to operate in the area as well.[74]

Eden displayed little support for the American plan to limit the activities of IPC. According to the foreign secretary, British oil companies had concessions in Abu Dhabi territory dating from 1936; thirteen years before the Saudis ever laid claim to the now-disputed territory. Therefore, to simply retain the status quo of the period before the Saudi claim, IPC had to continue to operate in the area. Eden maintained that Aramco had never been in the disputed area before and should not be allowed to enter at this point in the negotiations. In addition, Eden assured Washington that the United Kingdom had made it "abundantly clear" to the Saudi Arabian government that it would only contemplate receiving a new oil concession if Aramco agreed. Finally, Eden asked the State Department to restrain Aramco from entering the disputed zone.[75]

Dulles attempted to offer the British a face-saving device to allow for IPC to halt operations in the disputed zone. In May 1954 the State Department suggested that the British stop oil operations for the summer, which was a common practice in the Arabian heat. The British rejected this proposal, claiming that if IPC halted operations, they could hardly hope to resume them until the lengthy arbitration process reached its conclusion. The British believed that any concession to Saudi Arabia only brought more demands from Riyadh. In London's view, the Saudis had agreed to arbitration only because of the blockade of Buraimi, and therefore Britain needed to maintain its strong position.[76]

The disagreement over oil operations in the disputed zone nearly led to violence between British forces and American nationals. Great Britain had made it clear to the State Department that it not only opposed the idea of an Aramco incursion into the disputed territory but also would, in fact, stop Aramco by force if necessary.[77] The United States clearly wanted to avoid any incidents in the disputed zone. The State Department strongly urged Aramco, even if pressured by the Saudi government, not to make a move into disputed territory without at least consulting with Washington.[78] The United States also complained to the Saudis that Riyadh should not place Aramco and American citizens in such a confrontational situation.[79] Appealing to the British to be reasonable, Aramco and the State Department asked Sir Roger Makins to understand that the Aramco concession might be jeopardized if the company did comply with King Saud's demand to begin exploration. The British ambassador expressed little sympathy for Aramco's plight, telling the Americans that "while HMG shared [the] desire to avoid an incident . . . if an American Company . . . felt obliged to fall in with this kind of blackmail they were asking for trouble." However, Makins did add that in his opinion "hostilities against an American oil company appear, at this juncture in our affairs to be . . . rather fantastic."[80]

As fantastic as the possibility may have seemed to Makins, Foreign Office officials Selwyn Lloyd and Evelyn Shuckburgh urged Churchill to authorize the use of firearms against any group moving into an area that Abu Dhabi considered its undisputed territory.[81] Churchill wanted to overawe any Aramco party with a large force of Trucial Levies to avoid the use of firearms. As the prime minister explained to Selwyn Lloyd, "It is easy to write about shooting the wheel of a motor car and not injuring the American inside. Bullets are very rarely accurately directed. It would be a very unfortunate moment for the British to shoot an American citizen, even if his own government had asked him not to go where he had gone."[82] Eden approved Churchill's plan to use large numbers of troops to reduce the need to employ weapons, as long as it did not delay the removal of any Aramco oil party.[83]

Despite fears of a confrontation, the Aramco incursion ended peacefully. On June 5, 1954, RAF planes dropped leaflets on the party once it crossed into territory that Abu Dhabi claimed. The American oil team beat a hasty retreat to Saudi territory in less than a week, while still publicly maintaining their right to be in an area that Riyadh claimed as its own. The Levies sent to expel the Aramco party found only an empty camp.[84]

The Saudi government expressed its anger at what it saw as the failure of the United States to support its position. On June 1, 1954, Saudi Foreign Minister Prince Faisal held a meeting with Ambassador Wadsworth. The prince told Wadsworth that he understood that Britain and the United States needed to cooperate because of their common global interests, "but as one result, small though it was on the world plane, Saudi Arabia was the loser." As the United States had proved unwilling to help the Saudis, Riyadh would "no longer trouble [America] with its small problems but would henceforth handle them to the best of its abilities." As part of this new self-reliance, the prince added, Saudi Arabia intended to cancel the Point IV economic aid it received from Washington.[85] When asked by the State Department to reconsider the cancellation of aid, the Saudi government explained that "it all depended on the Buraimi question." The Saudi government clamed that it could not rely on the United States to help curb British "barbarism and aggression." Prince Faisal protested, "It was not a question of oil . . . . It was rather a question of [Saudi] prestige and [the] right to be treated on an equal footing." Riyadh could not accept the fact the United States advised it to accept the British arbitration proposal that would allow only British oil companies to continue operations.[86]

The Aramco incursion had the potential of causing a serious breach in Anglo-American relations, particularly as it came at the same time as the growing British fear over American involvement in Iraq and in the midst of the allies' disagreement over the course of the ongoing Geneva Conference on Indochina. Despite the danger of violence, Britain remained determined to expel the Aramco party by force. London's reaction demonstrates the lengths that Churchill's government was willing to go to defend its interests in the Persian Gulf from any challenge. Fear that the United States might be enraged by the injury of any American citizens prompted Churchill to be cautious but not to refrain from deploying force. The Conservative government did not act as if maintaining good Anglo-American relations was its primary goal in the Persian Gulf. For its part, Washington did not attempt to bully the British into a compromise. The State Department appealed to London to be reasonable about Aramco exploration in the disputed area, but never threatened the British with any consequence if they remained intransigent.

THE ARBITRATION AGREEMENT AND AFTERMATH

In early June 1954 Washington's patient council of both sides to reach a peaceful accord seemed finally to pay off. Discussions in Saudi Arabia between the British and American ambassadors led to a compromise on arbitration. American Ambassador Wadsworth told his British counterpart that the United States agreed to support all of Britain's arbitration points with the exception of exclusive IPC oil operations in the disputed zone. Wadsworth suggested a division of the disputed territory for the purposes of oil operations until arbitration decided the final borders. British Ambassador Pelham agreed with his American colleague and urged London to accept the American's plan. Pelham claimed that the United States would pressure the Saudis to accept "whatever reasonable division Her Majesty's Government might propose." In addition, he wrote that acceptance of the plan "would enable the Americans to redeem themselves with the Saudi Arabian Government . . . and I do not think we should underestimate the importance of this to them."[87] On June 12, 1954, London authorized Pelham to begin to negotiate with the Saudis along the lines he had proposed.[88] When Churchill and Eden visited Washington in late June 1954, the foreign secretary reassured an anxious John Foster Dulles that "the problem of arbitration was being worked out."[89]

On July 18, 1954, Pelham cabled the Foreign Office with an outline of the final arbitration agreement to cover both Buraimi and the general Saudi–Abu Dhabi frontier. Turki and his party, along with the British forces, would leave the Buraimi area and be replaced by a small police force made up of troops from both sides. Both parties agreed not to introduce any new troops into the disputed area and to allow the arbitration body to visit Buraimi to settle any dispute about the implementation of the agreement. Pending the completion of arbitration, the area in Abu Dhabi claimed by the Saudis in 1949 would be divided into three sections. IPC would continue to operate in one section, Aramco would be allowed to operate in a second area, and a neutral zone would divide the two oil companies.[90]

While Saudi Arabia had agreed to arbitration, it still harbored ill feelings toward the United States. In a meeting with Secretary of State Dulles in September 1954, the Saudi ambassador expressed the opinion that American assistance over the Buraimi dispute "could have been more effective."[91] Prince Faisal also complained about the American government's lack of support, quoting to an Aramco official an old Arab proverb, "There is no difference between a useless friend and a harmless enemy."[92]

Arbitration on the frontier question began in Geneva on January 22, 1955. The Arbitration Tribunal continued to meet during the remainder of Churchill's stay in office, but in October 1955 the process ended when the British representative and the neutral commissioners resigned over the issue of Saudi bribery of witnesses. On October 16, 1955, Prime Minister Anthony Eden ordered the British military to occupy the Buraimi Oasis and unilaterally declare a border. Eisenhower's administration protested but took no action against the United Kingdom. Britain and Saudi Arabia negotiated off and on until the Saudis broke diplomatic relations with London in the wake of the Suez invasion.[93] The border dispute did not come to a final conclusion until 1974 when Riyadh recognized Abu Dhabi's claim to the oasis after direct negotiations with the ruler of Abu Dhabi.[94]

CONCLUSION

The Buraimi dispute has attracted the attention of a number of historians interested primarily in Anglo-American relations in the Middle East. Ritchie Ovendale described the dispute as a conflict of interest between the United States and Great Britain. According to Ovendale, London believed that Washington's failure to unconditionally support its position would be taken as a sign in the Arab world that America intended to replace Britain in the Middle East. For its part, the United States government held the opinion that good relations with Saudi Arabia were of more importance to the overall Western position in the Middle East than Britain's support of its small Gulf allies.[95]

Tore Petersen's article on Buraimi in *International History Review* also points to an Anglo-American clash of interests. According to Petersen the Eisenhower administration placed more value on Saudi friendship than on the continuation of Britain's empire in the Middle East. Petersen believes that London's fear that America planned to replace Britain in the region was justified, as Washington felt compelled to fill what it saw as a void left by the decline of British power in the Middle East. The Eisenhower administration, therefore, sought to replace British oil firms with American companies wherever possible.[96] Petersen concluded that Britain's firm stance at Buraimi foreshadowed the Suez invasion that brought Anglo-American relations in the Middle East to their nadir.[97] Petersen refined his thesis in his book, *The Middle East between the Great Powers: Anglo-American Conflict and Cooperation, 1952–7*. In the larger work the author makes it clear that he does not believe that the United States actively conspired to weaken the British in the Middle East and would have preferred to see a less imperialistic Britain remain a power in the area. However, the Eisenhower administration believed that heavy-handed British imperialism was alienating the Arab world and creating an opportunity for Soviet influence to spread, therefore the United States felt compelled to replace Britain in order to contain Communism. For Petersen, the British intransigence at Buraimi so angered the Eisenhower White House that the Americans were more willing to act in a decisive manner against the British during the Suez Crisis.[98]

In a recent study of Saudi-American relations, historian Nathan Citino presents a different view of the Buraimi affair, portraying the United States as more supportive of the British than Ovendale or Petersen. Citino argues that Washington and London agreed that British domination of the Persian Gulf was vital to the overall Western plan to allow Western Europe to have a ready supply of oil and for Great Britain to remain economically viable through the exploitation of that oil. The major dispute between the two allies centered on their respective approaches on how to maintain the British position. The Eisenhower administration had great faith in the ability of private enterprises, like Aramco, to promote Western interests in the Middle East, while London still relied on the traditional imperial policies of protectorates and military force. While Washington tried to mediate between the British and Saudis, in the end, the Americans placed more value on propping up Great Britain than in placating Saudi Arabia.[99]

While all of these historians make some valid points, their interpretations also have some weaknesses. The view of the Buraimi dispute as a clash of interests between the United Kingdom and the United States is clearly well founded, but it is difficult to argue that the United States placed a greater value on Saudi friendship than it did on its alliance with Great Britain during the dispute or that America was maneuvering to replace the British in the Middle East. Citino's assertion that Washington supported the British as much as possible is correct, but London's fear of American intentions undercuts his claim that both allies understood that the British position in the Persian Gulf would be jointly protected. The determination of Churchill and Eden to stand up to Saudi aggression was not predicated on the idea that they would receive the assistance of the United States.

London's interest in protecting the rights of its Persian Gulf allies arose from two sources. The Gulf sheikhdoms had great value to Britain as oil producing regions with secure ties to London. The British were also motivated by a desire to stand up to Saudi Arabia. London feared that any further blow to the declining prestige of the British Empire in the Middle East could be fatal. London resisted compromise and employed force to blockade Buraimi because Churchill's government sought a victory over the Saudis as a symbol of British resolve to hold on in the Middle East. Although London recognized the terrible dilemma that Washington had been placed in, the British pursued a hard line with Riyadh. In spite of American concerns, when arbitration failed in late 1955, Prime Minister Eden settled the dispute with a unilateral use of force. Churchill's belligerent attitude during the dispute suggests that he would have taken similar action if arbitration had broken down while he still occupied 10 Downing Street.

Washington's position on the Buraimi dispute also arose from its overall national interests, which differed from those of Britain. The containment of Communism remained the Eisenhower administration's chief foreign policy concern. Therefore, during the Buraimi dispute, Washington tried to be the voice for compromise. The United States sought a solution that would alienate neither London nor Riyadh. The State Department attempted to act as an "honest broker" between its two friends, prodding them toward accommodation while trying to maintain a neutral stance. However, Washington's firm support for the basic British proposal of arbitration, despite angry protests by the Saudis, shows that it valued the British alliance more than Saudi friendship.

Any charge that the United States sought to diminish British power in the Persian Gulf during the Buraimi crisis does not stand up to scrutiny. Whatever Dulles may have privately thought about the long-term viability of the British Empire in the Middle East, the State Department resisted a great deal of pressure from Riyadh to support the Saudi position. Saudi-American relations suffered real, albeit temporary, damage as a result of Washington's perceived tilt toward Britain. The air base at Dhahran and the Aramco concession were both potentially threatened by Washington's refusal to support Saudi claims to the oasis. While London maintained its suspicion of American motivations in the Middle East, it would have been unrealistic for the British to expect any more support than they got from Washington. The United States could not completely turn its back on the Saudis if it hoped to maintain even a semblance of good relations with Riyadh. During Churchill's second ministry, despite London's fears of American neo-imperialism, Washington did not intended to replace the British in the Middle East. Rather, the Americans tried to mediate between the British and the Arabs in an attempt to secure the overall Western position in the region. London saw little threat from Communism in the Middle East, believing the chief danger to the Western position arose from Arab nationalism. The British mistook the American attempts to reconcile Arab nationalism and British imperialism as a betrayal. In fact, the United States gave the United Kingdom all the support it possibly could to defend its position in the Middle East without destroying the hopes of creating a wider "free world" alliance against the Communist threat.

As to the issue of oil, London pursued the interests of the British-based petroleum companies more keenly than Washington defended Aramco. The Foreign Office urged IPC to begin operations in the disputed zone after the end of the Standstill Agreement. London flatly refused to consider suspending these operations to reach an arbitration agreement and publicly called for the voluntary transfer of Saudi concessions to British companies. London did not even flinch from the possible use of violence against Aramco if it violated territory claimed by Abu Dhabi. On the other hand, the State Department proved quite willing to support the transfer of some oil concessions from Aramco to IPC in the disputed zone. When Aramco refused, State Department officials urged the company to reconsider, as they believed the company already had sufficient oil-producing territories. Although the State Department eventually supported Aramco's policy of not surrendering any of its concession, this does not indicate that Washington sought to expand the oil company's holdings at the expense of British firms.

Overall, the Buraimi dispute showcases the fact the Churchill's government maintained a commitment to defending the British Empire and British oil interests with or without American approval. The Eisenhower administration's main focus was on the containment of the Soviet Union. When these goals came into conflict, as they often did in the Middle East, they became a source of tension between London and Washington. However, in significant contrast to the post-Suez era, during the Buraimi dispute Great Britain was still able to pursue a policy that was quite independent of the United States. The Eisenhower administration showed a remarkable tolerance for British intransigence on the issue, as Washington had not yet given up on the hope that Britain would still be able to be the principal Western guardian of the Middle East. Of course, on a global scale the United States placed more value on London's friendship than that of Saudi Arabia's. Riyadh was at best a regional ally for Washington while Great Britain remained a formidable, albeit diminished, world power.

NOTES

1. PRO, FO 371/104294, April 18, 1953, "Saudi Arabian Frontier Dispute: Brief for the United Kingdom Delegation to the United Nations"; "Secret Security Information, Problem: UK-Saudi Arabian Dispute over Buraimi," January 16, 1953, 641.86A/11-852, State Department central files, record group 59, National Archives, College Park, Maryland.

2. Ritchie Ovendale, *Britain, the United States and the Transfer of Power in the Middle East, 1945–1962* (New York, 1996), 85–86; PRO, FO 371/104294, April 18, 1953, "Saudi Arabian Frontier Dispute: Brief for the United Kingdom Delegation to the United Nations."

3. Ovendale, *Transfer of Power*, 85–86; PRO FO 371/104294, May 1, 1953, Eastern Department minute "The Sultan of Muscat and Central Oman."

4. Irvine H. Anderson, *Aramco, The United States, and Saudi Arabia: A Study of the Dynamics of Foreign Oil Policy* (Princeton, NJ, 1981), ix–x, 30–34, 198–202; Ovendale, *Transfer of Power*, 27–28, 41–44; Gulshan Dietl, *The Dulles Era: America Enters West Asia* (New Delhi, 1986), 41–42.

5. PRO, FO 371/104275, January 7, 1953, "Foreign Office Intel to UK Missions Abroad."

6. PRO, FO 371/104276, January 9, 1953, Ministry of Defense to GHQ Middle East Land Forces.

7. PRO, FO 371/104276, January 15, 1953, Chiefs of Staff Committee meeting no. 24.

8. Andrew Fritzlan to Parker Hart, February 2, 1953, 641.86A/2-253, State Department central files, record group 59, National Archives, College Park, Maryland; FRUS 1952–1954 IX, p. 2515 (footnote to no. 1502), February 3, 1953, Raymond Hare to the State Department.

9. FRUS 1952–1954 IX, no. 1503, March 2, 1953, memorandum of conversation between Dulles and Faisal.

10. FRUS 1952–1954 IX, no. 1504, March 2, 1953, memorandum of conversation between Eisenhower, Dulles, and Faisal.

11. FRUS 1952–1954 IX, no. 1506, March 16, 1953, memorandum of conversation between Bedell Smith and Al Faqih.

12. Memorandum of conversation between Dulles and Faisal, March 23, 1953, 786A.11/5-2353, State Department central files, record group 59, National Archives, College Park, Maryland.

13. Henry Byroade, assistant secretary of state, to John Foster Dulles, secretary of state, March 24, 1953, 786A.11/3-2453, State Department central files, record group 59, National Archives, College Park, Maryland.

14. Memorandum of conversation between Bedell Smith and Faisal, March 25, 1953, 786A.11/3-2553, State Department central files, record group 59, National Archives, College Park, Maryland.

15. Office of Near Eastern Affairs memorandum on "Prince Faisal's Visit to the United States," April 13, 1953, 786A.11/4-553, State Department central files, record group 59, National Archives, College Park, Maryland.

16. John Jernegan, assistant deputy secretary of state to the secretary of defense, February 26, 1953, 786A.5 MSP/22053, State Department central files, record group 59, National Archives, College Park, Maryland.

17. PRO, PREM 11/698, March 6, 1953, Eden to Churchill.

18. PRO, FO 371/104280, March 7, 1953, Foreign Office to Eden.

19. PRO, FO 371/104285, March 17, 1953, Pelham to Bowker.

20. PRO, CAB 129/60, C. (53) 103, March 16, 1953, memorandum by Eden.

21. PRO, FO 371/104283, March 23, 1953, Foreign Office to Bahrain; FO 371/104283, March 26, 1953, Foreign Office to Bahrain; FO 371/104283, March 28, 1953, Eden to Makins.

22. PRO, FO 371/104286, March 31, 1953, Makins to the Foreign Office.

23. PRO, FO 371/104288, March 31, 1953, Foreign Office minute: record of conversation between Strang and Aldrich.

24. FRUS 1952–1954 IX, no. 1512, April 2, 1953, Dulles to Hare.

25. PRO, FO 371/104291, April 20, 1953, Foreign Office brief for the minister of state at NATO conference.

26. PRO, FO 371/104289, April 2, 1953, Foreign Office minute by Greenhill.

27. FRUS 1952–1954 IX, no. 1513, April 3, 1953, memorandum of conversation.

28. PRO, FO 371/104290, April 17, 1953, Foreign Office minute by Ross.

29. FRUS 1952–1954 IX, no. 1514, April 16, 1953, memorandum of conversation.

30. PRO, FO 371/104290, April 21, 1953, Pelham to the Foreign Office; FO 371/104290, April 23, 1953, Pelham to the Foreign Office; FO 371/104291, April 24, 1953, Pelham to the Foreign Office.

31. PRO, FO 371/104291, April 23, 1953, Strang to Churchill.

32. PRO, FO 371/104293, May 1, 1953, Churchill to Selwyn Lloyd.

33. PRO, FO 371/104293, May 2, 1953, Foreign Office to Pelham.

34. PRO, FO 371/104294, May 13, 1953, Pelham to the Foreign Office.

35. PRO, FO 371/104295, May 22, 1953, Lloyd to Churchill.

36. PRO, FO 317/104296, May 24, 1953, Churchill personal minute to Selwyn Lloyd.

37. PRO, FO 371/104296, May 1953, Lloyd personal minute to Churchill.

38. PRO, FO 371/104296, June 2, 1953, Foreign Office to Pelham.

39. PRO, FO 371/104297, June 9, 1953, Pelham to the Foreign Office.

40. Memorandum of conversation: Dulles and King Ibn Saud, May 18, 1953, State Department lot files, Executive Secretariat 1949–1963, conference files, Dulles-Stassen trip to the Middle East, record group 59, National Archives, College Park, Maryland.

41. Memorandum of conversation: Dulles and Crown Prince Saud, May 18, 1953, State Department lot files, Executive Secretariat 1949–1963, conference files, Dulles-Stassen trip to the Middle East, record group 59, National Archives, College Park, Maryland.

42. Memorandum of conversation: Dulles and Prince Faisal, May 19, 1953, State Department lot files, Executive Secretariat 1949–1963, conference files, Dulles-Stassen trip to the Middle East, record group 59, National Archives, College Park, Maryland.

43. John Foster Dulles Papers, Mudd Library, box 73, re: Middle East in 1952, personal and private, "Important Points of Trip."

44. Raymond Hare, ambassador to Saudi Arabia to the State Department, June 2, 1953, 611.86A/6-253; State Department central files, record group 59, National Archives, College Park, Maryland.

45. PRO, FO 371/104297, June 10, 1953, Beely to Bowker.

46. PRO, FO 371/104295, May 27, 1953, Bowker to Makins.

47. PRO, PREM 11/698, May 22, 1953, J. R. C. to Strang.

48. FRUS IX, no. 1518, June 24, 1953, memorandum by the director of the Policy Planning Staff.

49. PRO, FO 371/104299, June 26, 1953, Foreign Office minute by Greenhill.

50. Henry Byroade, assistant secretary of state, to John Foster Dulles, secretary of state, June 30, 1953, State Department miscellaneous lot files, subject files, Arabian Peninsula, record group 59, National Archives, College Park, Maryland.

51. PRO, CAB 21/3073, July 11, 1953, "Visit of the Most Honorable the Marquess of Salisbury, K. G., Acting Secretary of State for Foreign Affairs to Washington."

52. PRO, FO 371/104299, July 13, 1953, Foreign Office to Lord Salisbury; CAB 128/26, July 13, 1953, cc (53) 42nd conclusion, item 3.

53. PRO, CAB 21/3073, July 14, 1953, "Visit of the Most Honorable the Marquees of Salisbury, K. G., Acting Secretary of State for Foreign Affairs to Washington."

54. PRO, FO 371/104300, July 20, 1953, Foreign Office minute by Ross.

55. PRO, CAB 128/26, July 21, 1953, cc (53) 44th conclusion, item 5.

56. PRO, FO 371/104301, July 28, 1953, Salisbury to Dulles.

57. FRUS 1952–1954 IX, no. 1534, August 28, 1953, Dulles to Salisbury.

58. PRO, FO 371/104309, September 31, 1953, Foreign Office brief.

59. PRO, FO 371/104307, October 13, 1953, Eden to Dulles.

60. Evelyn Shuckburgh, *Descent to Suez: Diaries, 1951–56* (New York, 1986), 105.

61. PRO, PREM 11/718, May 13, 1953, Pelham to the Foreign Office.
62. PRO, FO 371/104306, September 21, 1953, Foreign Office minute by Bowker.
63. PRO, CAB 128/27, January 7, 1954, cc (54) 1st conclusion, 6th item.
64. FRUS 1952–1954 IX, no. 1540, November 6, 1953, Chargé D'Affaires Jones to the State Department.
65. PRO, FO 371/109829, February 11, 1954, Selwyn Lloyd to Eden; FO 371/109829, February 12, 1954, Eden to Selwyn Lloyd.
66. FRUS 1952–1954 IX, no. 1543, February 15, 1954, Foreign Office to American Embassy, London.
67. FRUS 1952–1954 IX, no. 1545, February 16, 1954, Bedell Smith to the American Embassy, Saudi Arabia; PRO, FO 371/109829, February 16, 1954, Beeley to Fry.
68. FRUS, 1952–1954 IX, no. 1546, March 9, 1954, Wadsworth to the State Department.
69. FRUS, 1952–1954 IX, no. 1547, March 9, 1954, Wadsworth to the State Department.
70. FRUS, 1952–1954 IX, no. 1548, March 10, 1954, memorandum of conversation.
71. FRUS, 1952–1954 IX, no. 1550, March 16, 1954, Dulles to the American Embassy in Saudi Arabia.
72. FRUS 1952–1954 IX, no. 1553, March 19, 1954, Wadsworth to the State Department; PRO, FO 371/109830, March 21, 1954, Pelham to the Foreign Office.
73. FRUS 1942–1954 IX, March 23, 1954, memorandum of conversation.
74. PRO, FO 371/109831, April 14, 1954, Beely to Fry.
75. FRUS 1952–1954 IX, no. 1560, April 29, 1954, Bedell Smith to Wadsworth.
76. PRO, FO 371/109833, May 18, 1954, Foreign Office minute by Fry.
77. FRUS 1952–1954 IX, no. 1564, May 24, 1954, Aldrich to the State Department.
78. FRUS 1952–1954 IX, no. 1560, April 29, 1954, Bedell Smith to Wadsworth.
79. PRO, FO 371/109833, May 27, 1954, Foreign Office to British Delegation at Geneva.
80. PRO, FO 371/109833, May 25, 1954, Makins to the Foreign Office.
81. Shuckburgh, *Descent to Suez*, 217; PRO, FO 800/808, June 2, 1954, Lloyd to Churchill.
82. PRO, FO 371/109834, June 2, 1954, Churchill to Lloyd.
83. PRO, CAB 128/27, June 5, 1954, cc (54), 39th conclusion, item 4.
84. FRUS 1952–1954 IX, no. 1566, June 6, 1954, Wadsworth to the State Department; PRO, FO 371/109834, June 15, 1954, Burrows to the Foreign Office.
85. FRUS 1952–1954 IX, no. 1563, June 1, 1954, Wadsworth to the State Department.
86. United States Embassy, Jidda to John Foster Dulles, secretary of state, June 4, 1954, 611.86A/6-454, State Department central files, record group 59, National Archives, College Park, Maryland.
87. PRO, FO 371/109834, June 5, 1954, Pelham to the Foreign Office.
88. PRO, FO 371/109835, June 12, 1954, Foreign Office to Pelham.

89. FRUS 1952–1954 IX, no. 468, June 25, 1954, memorandum of White House meeting.

90. PRO, FO 371/109838, July 18, 1954, Pelham to the Foreign Office, "Exchange of Letters Saudis Will Accept."

91. FRUS 1952–1954 IX, no. 1464, September 25, 1954, memorandum of conversation.

92. Record of a conversation between Prince Faisal and H. Jerry Corson and Frederik Awalt, August 31, 1954, 611.86A/8-3154, State Department central files, record group 59, National Archives, College Park, Maryland.

93. Tore Petersen, "Anglo-American Rivalry in the Middle East: The Struggle for the Buraimi Oasis, 1952–57," *International History Review* 14 (February 1992): 84–86.

94. Dietl, *The Dulles Era*, 44.

95. Ovendale, *Transfer of Power*, 86–88.

96. Petersen, "Buraimi Oasis," 72–74.

97. Petersen, "Buraimi Oasis," 89.

98. Tore Petersen, *The Middle East between the Great Powers: Anglo-American Conflict and Cooperation, 1952–7* (New York, 2000), 74–75.

99. Nathan Citino, *From Arab Nationalism to OPEC: Eisenhower, King Saud and the Making of U.S.-Saudi Relations* (Indianapolis, 2002), 85, 161.

Chapter Five

On the Brink in East Asia: The First Offshore Islands Crisis

Great Britain and the United States pursued different agendas in East Asia just as they did in other parts of the globe. The issue of Western relations with the People's Republic of China and the question of the best method of containing Communism in Asia were at the heart of Anglo-American disagreements in the region. The so-called First Offshore Islands Crisis in 1954–1955 accentuated the depth of the differences in the policies of the United States and the United Kingdom in East Asia. An examination of the crisis will provide some insights as to how successful Britain was in following a foreign policy independent of the United States in East Asia, the amount of influence that London had over American policy, and Washington's reaction to its ally's reluctance to fully cooperate with American plans, particularly in regard to China.

The roots of Anglo-American differences over China policy began before Churchill returned to power in 1951. In 1950, under Attlee's Labor government, Great Britain had recognized the People's Republic of China (PRC) and had withdrawn recognition from the Nationalist regime on Taiwan. The Attlee government had concluded that a good relationship with the new government in Beijing constituted the best method of safeguarding the valuable colony of Hong Kong from Communist aggression. London also faced political pressure from its commonwealth partners in Asia to recognize the PRC. India, in particular, wished to have friendly relations with the new government of China. In terms of Cold War strategy, London believed that fostering good relations with Beijing would facilitate a diplomatic split between the Chinese and the Soviet Union. Churchill, while leader of the opposition, had supported Labor's China policy. When the Conservatives returned to power, they continued to follow a similar path in East Asia.[1]

Unlike the British, the Truman administration had taken a hard line with the Chinese Communists. While Secretary of State Dean Acheson believed, as did the British, that a wedge could be driven between Beijing and Moscow, Washington did not opt for recognition of Mao's government. A number of factors contributed to the divergence of America's stance from that of London. Domestic political concerns constrained Truman's China policy, as a powerful "China Lobby" pressed for continued American support for Chiang Kai-shek. Unlike Great Britain, the United States had few business interests in China, and therefore had limited economic reasons to recognize Beijing. Finally, Washington traditionally had a less pragmatic view of diplomatic recognition than London. The United States saw recognition as a stamp of approval, and the America public was in no mood to reward the Chinese Communists for their victory over the Nationalists.[2]

Although Sino-British relations were warmer than Sino-American relations, London and Beijing still had serious disagreements. London's failure to support the inclusion of the PRC in the United Nations caused Beijing the most distress. The PRC expressed its displeasure with London by delaying the implementation of full diplomatic relations following recognition.[3] The outbreak of the Korean War in June 1950 further strained Sino-British relations. The United Kingdom supported the American-led UN military intervention, and the commonwealth sent troops to Korea. However, Anglo-American cooperation in Korea did have its limits. Once the war had degenerated into a stalemate, Churchill's government placed a great deal of pressure on the Eisenhower administration to avoid an expansion of the fighting. London also pressed Washington to compromise with the Communists on the issue of forced repatriation of POWs to facilitate an armistice. Under pressure, the Americans dropped their demand that prisoner repatriation be completely voluntary.[4]

With the end of the Korean War in the summer of 1953, Britain moved to repair its relations with Beijing and return to its policy of seeking a modus vivendi with the PRC. The British were not unmindful of the need to maintain the security of their colonies and commonwealth partners in Asia from Communist expansion. Indeed, the British were at the time engaged in fighting against the Communist insurgency in Malaya. However, London did not share Washington's fear that Communism would spread rapidly throughout the region, with one nation after another falling in a "domino effect."[5] The Americans, on the other hand, became more determined than ever after the Korean War to support the Chinese Nationalists and funnel aid to the French in Indochina in order to contain the perceived threat from the Chinese Communists.[6]

The defeat of the French in Indochina and the Geneva Accords of 1954 only served to widen the gap between the United States and Great Britain over East Asian policy. The British had refused to consider a joint military intervention in Indochina with the Americans to save the French at Dien Bien Phu. Anthony Eden served as a prime architect of the Geneva Accords, which were very unpopular in Washington. The United States, which refused to sign the accords, considered the agreement to divide Vietnam a Communist victory and redoubled its efforts at containment. While Dulles harbored hopes of driving a wedge between Beijing and Moscow, he hoped to achieve this goal by firmly standing up to any aggression by the PRC. Dulles believed that in the long run the Soviet Union would distance itself from its more reckless Communist ally rather than risk being drawn into a war with the United States to save Beijing. Unlike Washington's relationship with Beijing, during the course of the Geneva negotiations Sino-British relations had improved. Eden and Chinese Foreign Minister Zhou Enlai had met privately several times in Geneva, as a result of which London and Beijing formalized relations by exchanging diplomatic representatives.[7]

With the situation in East Asia very tense, the First Offshore Islands Crisis only added fuel to the fire. Since the defeat of the Nationalists on the mainland in 1949, Chiang Kai-shek's forces had continued to occupy a number of islands in the Taiwan Straits very close to the mainland. The most important Nationalist positions included the Quemoy, Matsu, and Tachen island groups. While the United Kingdom considered these islands to be part of the PRC, Washington supported their continued control by Taiwan. The offshore islands had been effectively neutralized at the start of the hostilities in Korea when President Truman had ordered the Seventh Fleet to patrol the Taiwan Straits to prevent fighting between the Nationalists and Beijing. Eisenhower had modified this policy in February 1954 to allow for Chiang's forces to launch attacks on the mainland while still maintaining the Seventh Fleet as a shield for Taiwan. No longer constrained by the United States, the Nationalists began air and sea operations against mainland targets and shipping in the Taiwan Straits.[8] In the spring of 1954, when the People's Liberation Army (PLA) began retaliatory measures that seemed to threaten the offshore islands, Chiang Kai-shek sought an American commitment to help defend his forward bases. At this point, Eisenhower and Dulles expressed reluctance to publicly commit the United States to the defense of the offshore islands. Washington wanted to avoid the commitment of resources and prestige that a full-scale defense would entail. Dulles suggested to Taipei that the mere presence of the Seventh Fleet in the area provided sufficient deterrent to Beijing to safeguard the offshore islands.[9] This cautious stance by the United States would change over the coming months, and America and the People's Republic of China moved dangerously close to war. As the crisis developed, Washington sought to secure the support of its allies, particularly Great Britain, while London urged moderation on its American friends and sought to bring stability to East Asia.

THE CRISIS BEGINS

On September 3, 1954, heavy fighting flared in the Taiwan Straits for the first time when the PLA began an intensive shelling of Quemoy. The American navy quickly moved substantial forces, including three carriers, into position just off the island.[10] At the time of the attack, Secretary of State Dulles was in Manila furthering Washington's plans for containment in Asia by finalizing the creation of the South East Asian Treaty Organization (SEATO). Dulles expressed grave concern over the Communist attack on the island. He cabled Washington with a warning that the "loss of Quemoy would have grave psychological repercussions" and seriously damage the morale of the anti-Communist nations in Asia.[11] However, Dulles added an important note of caution. He argued that the United States should only commit itself to the defense of Quemoy if it seemed militarily feasible to hold the island in the face of a massive PLA assault. Comparing the situation to Dien Bien Phu, Dulles warned against repeating "the French mistake of making a symbol of what cannot be held."[12] Eisenhower concurred that it might be very difficult for the Nationalists to hold Quemoy, even with American military support.[13] The president also wanted to avoid any "possibility of driving a wedge between ourselves and our principal European allies, especially Britain," by making a unilateral decision to use force in the Taiwan Straits.[14] Dulles agreed that an American defense of Quemoy, which might require the use of atomic weapons, would alienate the European allies. The secretary of state also believed that Australia and New Zealand, Commonwealth States who were militarily tied to Washington in the Australia–New Zealand–United States (ANZUS) pact, would reject the use of force.[15] Anxious to avoid the loss of Quemoy, but equally concerned about the consequences of defending the island, Dulles suggested at a National Security Council meeting on September 12, 1954, that the issue be raised in the United Nations Security Council. The goal would be to effect the official neutralization of the offshore islands, or at least a temporary cease-fire.[16]

The administration's belief that London would be agitated about the possibility of American military action in the Taiwan Straits was well founded. On September 15, 1954, Dulles held a conversation with Sir Roger Makins in which he warned the British ambassador about the possibility of fighting between American and PLA forces. The secretary of state asked for a meeting with Foreign Secretary Eden to discuss the possibility of a UN-sponsored cease-fire or some other peaceful means of settling the dispute. Makins made no comment on the UN suggestion but warned Dulles that "as far as British opinion was concerned, there was all the difference between action to prevent or resist an attack on Formosa and intervention to hold an island so close to the Chinese mainland." Makins insisted that public opinion in the United Kingdom would never support a war over the offshore islands.[17]

Makins's comments to Dulles accurately reflected his government's position. The Foreign Office believed that the decision of whether or not to defend Quemoy could not be simply a military matter, as the "repercussions on Hong Kong and the [British] position in the Far East as a whole" needed to be taken into consideration. Whitehall wanted the Americans to keep it informed of any possible military action and urged Washington to restrain the Nationalists.[18] Churchill, supported by the British Chiefs of Staff, believed that the offshore islands were not vital to the defense of Taiwan. The prime minister hoped that the islands might be permanently neutralized.[19]

On September 17, 1954, per his request, Dulles met with Eden at the Foreign Office in London. Dulles reported that, while the United States had made no decision about the use of force, most American military advisers favored that option. The secretary of state said that the loss of Quemoy, coming so close after the Geneva Accords, would be a powerful signal that the United States could no longer be counted on to resist Communism in Asia. However, he admitted that the possibility existed of sparking a general war between the United States, the PRC, and the Soviet Union, if America used force to defend the islands. After painting this bleak picture, Dulles raised the suggestion of asking the United Nations Security Council to call for a cease-fire, which would, in effect, neutralize the offshore islands. Dulles argued that by bringing the issue to the UN, in case war broke out, the onus would then be placed on the Communists if the USSR and the PRC rejected the call for a cease-fire. As a final incentive to get Eden to agree, Dulles said that a cease-fire might lead to "a process of far-reaching negotiations . . . which could lead to a settlement of the present chaotic situation in the Far East." Eden told Dulles that he would consider his idea but suggested direct talks between Washington and Beijing. Dulles countered that direct talks would be politically infeasible for the administration and that even the UN plan had its critics in Washington.[20]

While the Dulles-Eden meeting had ended inconclusively, the secretary of state received Whitehall's answer a few days later. On September 22, 1954, Sir Pierson Dixon, British representative to the UN, met with Dulles in New York and conveyed Eden's general support for the Security Council proposal. However, the British had certain questions that they wanted to raise before proceeding. Eden believed that the PRC had to be invited to participate in the Security Council discussion of Quemoy. The foreign secretary also wanted to know if the United States would seek UN military intervention if Beijing refused to cooperate. Dulles assured Dixon that Beijing would be invited to send representatives. The secretary of state said that, while the United States would at this point only seek a cease-fire from the UN, he would not speculate as to what course of action America would take if the Communists derailed the proposal. Dulles reminded the British that there was still no guarantee that Chiang Kai-shek would agree to a cease-fire. In that case the plan would have to be abandoned before the Communists even learned of its existence. Finally, Dulles said that he wanted to ensure British cooperation before he raised the issue with Taipei.[21]

Eden and Dulles next met in London in late September at the Nine-Power Conference. While Eden had convened this meeting of the Western allies to discuss the entry of West Germany into NATO, he and Dulles took the opportunity to further discuss the details of the UN cease-fire proposal. Eden stressed the fact that the fighting in the Taiwan Straits had to be presented to the Security Council not as an act of Communist aggression but as a danger to world peace. Britain and the other states that recognized the PRC would find it difficult to characterize an armed attempt by Beijing to recapture the offshore islands as aggression, as they were clearly part of mainland China. In addition, Eden suggested that New Zealand present the Security Council proposal, in order to give both Washington and London more of a disinterested appearance.[22]

By September 30, 1954, Washington, London, and Wellington had agreed upon the basic outline of the cease-fire proposal, referred to as Operation "Oracle" by the British. At a time to be agreed upon by the three allies, New Zealand would present the proposal to the Security Council. In the meantime certain details would have to be worked out.[23]

It is clear that at the beginning of the Offshore Islands Crisis Washington and London cooperated closely to devise "Oracle" as a peaceful method of resolving the problem. In the first month of the crisis the United States clearly took the opinion of the United Kingdom into consideration before making any decisions. Washington fully apprised London of its plans even before discussing any options with Taipei. For their part, the British made no secret of the fact that they would find it almost impossible to support military action by the United States in defense of Quemoy. By agreeing to approach the UN on the issue, the British had helped Washington to avoid a hasty military response. While Dulles had argued to his American colleagues that a war with the PRC over Quemoy might not be in the best interests of the United States, it must have been easier for him to persuade hard-liners in the administration to accept a peaceful solution with the backing of London. In fact, Dulles placed such importance on the support of Britain that he offered the possibility of a wider settlement growing out of "Oracle" to entice Eden to go along with the plan. However, events would prove that Dulles was not sincere in his desire to seek a general agreement to reduce tensions in East Asia.

THE DEBATE OVER THE SCOPE OF "ORACLE"

Although the general outlines of the UN plan had been agreed to, the allies still needed to come to a consensus on the details. On October 2, 1954, in a meeting with Dulles in London, Eden raised two concerns about "Oracle." The foreign secretary requested that Moscow and Beijing be informed in advance about the UN proposal, although he believed that a few hours' warning would be sufficient. Dulles agreed to this suggestion. However, Eden's second question could not be disposed of so easily. Both Britain and New Zealand hoped that the proposed cease-fire would cover all fighting between the Nationalists and Communists and not be confined to Quemoy. The secretary of state told Eden that a total cease-fire would not be possible at the onset of "Oracle," as the Nationalists would never agree to this. Dulles did hold out the hope that once the fighting on the offshore islands stopped, a complete halt to the hostilities might be implemented.[24] These questions were not settled at the meeting, and over the next ten days the scope, and eventual goal, of "Oracle" became hotly contested issues between London and Washington. This debate demonstrates how the two allies were pursuing very different aims in East Asia.

After his return to Washington, Dulles began to meet with a small "working group" of British and New Zealand officials to work out the details of "Oracle." Dulles pointedly warned his allies that war might be inevitable if the UN operation failed. In Washington's opinion, as long as the PRC maintained that it would retake Taiwan by force, an attack on the offshore islands would be seen as a stepping-stone to an invasion of Taiwan. Dulles declared that such an invasion would "inevitably lead to a general war between the US and China."[25] After stressing the vital importance of "Oracle" in maintaining peace, Dulles said that the United States wanted the allies to agree to limit the UN operation to the fighting on Quemoy. Dulles wanted an agreement that the allies would avoid any discussion of broader issues, such as sovereignty over Taiwan or Chinese representation in the UN, when presenting "Oracle" to the Security Council. He argued that the Communists would undoubtedly try to raise these contentious issues. Dulles believed that if this were allowed to happen, it would publicly highlight the "embarrassing differences" between the United States and Great Britain over China policy.[26]

The British were dismayed by the American plan to limit "Oracle" to the Quemoy area. Sir Pierson Dixon reported to the Foreign Office that a narrow cease-fire would never be acceptable to the Soviets or the Chinese. In this case, the UN operation would only serve to publicly commit the United States to the defense of the offshore islands and expose an Anglo-American rift on the subject.[27] Minister of State Anthony Nutting informed Eden that he believed that

"Oracle" seemed to be diverging from its original concept as a step toward wider negotiations and should be reevaluated.[28] On October 8, 1954, the British Embassy expressed Eden's growing displeasure to the State Department. Eden rejected the restrictions on "Oracle" as a hindrance to his hopes for a general peace in East Asia. Eden admitted that his original attraction to the idea of a UN resolution arose from Dulles's claim that it would be a step on the road to broader negotiations. He argued that a local cease-fire would have the effect of maintaining the Nationalists on the offshore islands and would therefore appear to be an obvious "Cold-War gambit" by the United States. The foreign secretary offered a compromise. To avoid a general discussion by the UN of the problems of the two Chinas, Eden said he would be willing to limit the initial "Oracle" proposal to the offshore islands. However, Britain had to be at liberty to support a full cease-fire if another member raised the idea in the Security Council.[29]

On October 9, 1954, Dulles met with Sir Robert Scott of the British Embassy and New Zealand Ambassador Sir Leslie Munro. Munro said that his government concurred with London's assessment that limiting the scope of "Oracle" could not be seen as a positive step toward fostering the wider negotiations that Dulles had promised to consider back in September. Dulles tried to downplay his earlier suggestion that the UN proposal might be the beginning of broader discussions with Beijing. He said the cease-fire resolution was not meant as a first step in negotiations per se, but it would create a peaceful atmosphere in which the wider issues could be negotiated at a later date. Dulles said the United States could not agree to plunge into full-scale negotiations at this point. While he acknowledged that this was not what London and Wellington had in mind for "Oracle," he asked that his allies understand that the United States could not change its position. Dulles suggested that the allies agree to a diplomatic minute that would oblige them to oppose any expansion of the discussion beyond a cease-fire for the Quemoy area. As a concession to British opinion, Dulles agreed to add a clause that would allow the three governments to suggest a widening of the cease-fire beyond Quemoy if the Security Council first adopted the original narrow resolution.[30]

The next day the British raised several objections. The proposed minute still seemed too restrictive to Eden. The British wanted to be sure that "Oracle" did not appear designed only to benefit Taiwan by securing their possession of the islands. Furthermore, if the Communists did not cooperate with the resolution, the British wanted the Americans to understand that London would not commit to take further action. Dulles placated the British by assuring them that "Oracle" would be publicly presented as a strictly neutral idea to preserve world peace, not as assistance to the Nationalists. He agreed that the British were in no way bound to take any action if the Communists rejected "Oracle." As to the restrictive nature of the minute, Dulles said he realized that the wider issues of sovereignty and UN representation were bound to be raised in the Security Council and that he did not expect Britain to refrain from discussing them. He only wanted a promise that the allies would not take any action on the broader matters.[31] On October 12, 1954, Eden reluctantly recommended to the Cabinet that they accept the minute restricting "Oracle." The foreign secretary did not express great enthusiasm, telling his colleagues that the "whole plan was fraught with serious dangers, but the alternatives were even more alarming."[32] Apparently, Eden believed that it was better to accept a flawed plan rather than give up any influence on American actions in the Taiwan Straits.

The debate over the scope of "Oracle" demonstrates how Washington and London attempted to pressure each other to change their respective policies. Dulles was forced to reveal the lack of sincerity of his earlier promise to treat "Oracle" as the first step in wider negotiations. It seems likely that he had never intended to begin broad negotiations with Beijing. Dulles knew that Eden would be tempted by the suggestion of promoting a general settlement into cooperating on "Oracle." Even when his lack of honesty was revealed, Dulles still managed to convince the British to stay on board the project. A cease-fire that left the offshore islands in Chiang's hand would fulfill the American desire not to back down to Beijing while still avoiding a possible global war. Eden, on the other hand, wanted to ensure that "Oracle" would not become a simple Cold War ploy to paint the PRC as the aggressor in the Taiwan Straits. Faced with the prospect that the United States would become embroiled in a general war with China if no peaceful solution could be found, London decided to compromise on the scope of "Oracle" in order to continue to have some moderating effect on Washington. Neither of the two allies had changed their basic position on the offshore islands, but at this point they were willing to try to work together to find a peaceful solution.

U.S.-TAIWAN MUTUAL SECURITY PACT

While London and Washington had agreed to the details of Operation "Oracle" by mid-October 1954, the presentation of the resolution ran into serious delays. This was largely due to the decision of the United States to negotiate a mutual defense treaty with the Chinese Nationalists. Chiang Kai-shek's government had been pressing Washington for a formal alliance since the end of the Korean War. The Far Eastern Affairs Bureau of the State Department, along with the Joint Chiefs of Staff, supported the signing of a treaty. While Dulles supported the idea of a formal alliance, he resisted beginning negotiations because he felt a treaty would be unpopular with Britain and France. Dulles also told the Nationalists that as long as there were any hostilities in the Taiwan Straits, it would be difficult for the United States to sign a treaty with an active belligerent. The large-scale PLA attacks on the offshore islands, and the administration's desire to defuse the situation at the UN made Dulles reevaluate his stance. By early October 1954, unbeknownst to London, Dulles and Eisenhower had concluded that in order to get Chiang to accept the "Oracle" plan, he would have to be offered a mutual security treaty by Washington. The administration also hoped that the terms of any such treaty would have the added benefit of keeping the Nationalists from taking any further aggressive actions against the mainland. As Dulles suspected, on October 12, 1954, when Washington finally informed Taipei about "Oracle," Chiang denounced the idea and demanded a mutual defense treaty that would include the offshore islands.[33]

During the course of the negotiations in October and November 1954, the United States offered to formally include Taiwan and the adjacent Pescadores in the treaty, but there was no mention of the offshore islands. However, the Americans agreed to include a vague clause that stipulated that other territories could be added to the scope of the treaty at any time by mutual agreement. The United States intended this purposefully obscure reference to the offshore islands to act as a deterrent to a Chinese Communist attack without specifically pledging America to the defense of the islands. Washington also demanded that Taipei agree not to launch any offensive operations against the mainland without prior American authorization. This last addendum to the treaty would be handled by a separate exchange of notes following the signing of the main agreement.[34]

On October 14, 1954, the State Department informed Sir Roger Makins of Washington's plan to conclude a U.S.-Taiwan treaty. Dulles's message said that Chiang's reluctance to cooperate on "Oracle" necessitated the treaty, although Taipei had promised no quid pro quo. The secretary of state also pointed out that the treaty, which had been contemplated for some time, would help solidify the Western defensive position in the Pacific. Dulles believed that London should not object to the treaty as it was defensive in nature, did not include the offshore islands, and did not allow Chiang to attack the mainland from a safe haven on Taiwan. Dulles hoped that Britain would agree to launch "Oracle" before the existence of the U.S.-Taiwan treaty was announced.[35]

Whitehall refused to swallow the treaty and move on with the UN resolution. Eden quickly cabled Makins with instructions to inform the State Department that there would be no Security Council action until London had a clear picture of the nature of the U.S.-Taiwan treaty. Eden questioned the value of the treaty, pointing out that the United States had already publicly guaranteed the security of Taiwan and defended it with the Seventh Fleet. If news of the treaty leaked, which Eden believed was bound to happen, "Oracle" would seem like a ploy to bloodlessly keep the offshore islands in Nationalist hands.[36]

On October 18, 1954, Dulles tried to quiet the concerns of the United Kingdom. He told Makins that the treaty with Taipei was necessary because the orders of the Seventh Fleet to protect Taiwan were issued during the Korean War and might not be considered constitutionally valid now that the war was over. Dulles reassured the British that the treaty would not be extended to cover the offshore islands. The object of the treaty, according to Dulles, was to place the Chinese Nationalists in the same position as the South Koreans and West Germans. In other words, Chiang would not have to formally renounce his claim to Communist-held territory, but he would be constrained from taking any military action to accomplish a reconquest. Dulles pressed the British to move ahead with "Oracle." He argued that if the UN neutralized the offshore islands, this would facilitate London's goal of a stable East Asia.[37]

Despite Dulles's failure to get the United Kingdom to agree to launch "Oracle" while he concluded the negotiations with the Nationalists, he moved ahead with the treaty. On November 23, 1954, the State Department confidentially informed the British that Taipei and Washington had finished negotiations on the pact. Dulles again stressed the facts that the offshore islands were not specifically included in the treaty and that the Nationalists could not take offensive action without Washington's approval.[38] Eden replied that the proposed treaty did not meet the requirements that London had set for continuation with "Oracle." Specifically, the treaty did not explicitly bar Chiang from taking offensive action against the mainland in the future, nor did it clearly state that the United States would not take part in any defense of the offshore islands. Eden considered that the U.S.-Taiwan treaty had "radically changed" the nature of the proposed UN cease-fire, and he concluded that Britain could not agree to support the treaty nor proceed with "Oracle" unless Dulles made a public statement addressing London's concerns.[39] Dulles would not agree to the British conditions. He warned that a failure to begin "Oracle" might endanger world peace. Despite this dire warning, the most that the allies could agree to was to review the situation after the public announcement of the mutual defense treaty had been made.[40]

The official signing of the defensive treaty between the United States and Taiwan occurred on December 2, 1954. Predictably, the People's Republic of China denounced the agreement. Beijing accused London of collaborating with the United States to prop up the Nationalist regime.[41] London quickly announced that the treaty was strictly a matter between Washington and

Taipei. The British pointed to the defensive nature of the pact and urged all the parties involved in the offshore islands dispute to remain calm and seek a peaceful solution.[42]

The United States and Great Britain soon returned to negotiations about the launching of Operation "Oracle." On December 6, 1954, Dulles told Makins and New Zealand Ambassador Munro that he wanted to move forward on "Oracle" very soon, as he believed that the announcement of the treaty had gone smoothly. Makins told Dulles that Eden believed that "Oracle" had to be delayed. He pointed out that the PRC was unlikely to cooperate in a cease-fire because of its extreme displeasure with the treaty. Makins said that, in any case, under the present circumstances a local cease-fire did not seem to be advancing the cause of a wider settlement in East Asia. The British believed that "Oracle" might only further anger the Chinese Communists. Dulles continued to push for the UN resolution, claiming that simply raising the issue of the offshore islands in the Security Council would have a restraining effect on Beijing, even if the measure was not brought to a vote.[43] Partly swayed by this argument, Eden agreed to talk the issue over with Dulles in Paris during an upcoming NATO meeting.[44]

At Paris, Eden tried to convince the secretary of state that the current diplomatic atmosphere would make "Oracle" unworkable. Not only had the U.S.-Taiwan treaty upset Beijing but also, in mid-November, the Communists had sentenced thirteen American airmen captured in China during the Korean War to prison for espionage. UN Secretary General Hammarskjold had plans to travel to Beijing to seek their release in January, and Eden wanted to await the outcome of this trip before reconsidering "Oracle." Dulles agreed, believing that the situation in the Taiwan Straits seemed to have calmed down for the moment, making a cease-fire less urgent.[45]

Dulles had tried, and failed, to force the United Kingdom to agree to launch "Oracle" before the world learned of the new American treaty with Taiwan. In Washington the treaty and "Oracle" were related to the overall goals of easing tension in the Taiwan Straits while at the same time maintaining the Nationalist occupation of the offshore islands. Of course, London could not stop the United States from signing a military pact with Taiwan. However, London simply refused to be a party to the American plan to spring the U.S.-Taiwan treaty on the world after a cease-fire had been established. London clearly saw that, under these conditions, having the UN try to impose a cease-fire on the offshore islands did not constitute a meaningful step toward broader negotiations. As the British would not cooperate on the issue of the treaty, and Washington knew it could not go forward in the UN without the support of London, "Oracle" remained on the shelf. America would not be able to easily achieve its dual goals in the Taiwan Straits if Britain pursued a separate agenda.

THE CRISIS HEATS UP: JANUARY 1955

On January 10, 1955, the temporary calm in the Taiwan Straits disappeared. Hundreds of PLA aircraft raided the Nationalist positions on the Tachen islands, located more than three hundred miles north of Quemoy. On January 18 PLA forces captured Yijiang Island, located just north of the Tachens. Eisenhower believed that the Tachens, which could not be covered from the Nationalist air bases on Taiwan, should be evacuated. These events seem to have made Dulles more hawkish on the issue of the offshore islands. The secretary of state and Admiral Arthur Radford, chairman of the Joint Chiefs of Staff, urged Eisenhower to publicly state that the United States would come to the defense of Quemoy and the Matsus once the Tachens were evacuated. As Eisenhower planned to ask Congress for formal authorization to use force to defend Taiwan, Dulles urged that he take the opportunity to clearly state that Quemoy and the Matsus were to come under American military protection.[46]

On January 20, 1955, Dulles informed Makins of these new initiatives. He told the ambassador that, in order to offset the damage to Nationalist morale that the evacuation of the Tachens would cause, guarantees would have to be given for the other offshore islands. Dulles said that the guarantee would be provisional, not a permanent addition to the U.S.-Taiwan treaty. If Beijing accepted the de facto independence of Taiwan and the Pescadores from the mainland, or the UN negotiated a cease-fire, than the American commitment would be abandoned. Under the current circumstances Dulles proposed that "Oracle" be launched as soon as possible to reduce the possibility of the outbreak of war.[47]

London did not readily accept the American proposal. Eden cabled Makins with his displeasure. "I find these developments disturbing," he wrote. "Our ultimate objective, and I have always understood that it was Dulles's as well, had been to try to separate Formosa and the Pescadores from the coastal islands. We want to see the Nationalists abandon all these islands because so long as they occupy them there will be continuing danger of friction and fighting." While Eden saw the evacuation of the Tachens as a positive step, he believed that Beijing would never accept any of the coastal islands remaining in Chiang's hands in the long run. The foreign secretary feared that the "provisional guarantee" of which Dulles spoke would become a permanent American commitment. It seemed highly unlikely that the PRC would publicly agree to the political separation of Taiwan from the mainland, nor was Beijing liable to accept any UN cease-fire. Eden, while still hoping for a UN solution, did not believe that if the United States guaranteed Quemoy, then Britain should go forward with "Oracle." Finally, the foreign secretary questioned the wisdom of defending Quemoy, as Dulles had earlier said in public that the United States would have to use atomic weapons to do so.[48] Eden was correct to worry about nuclear escalation, for while Eisenhower and Dulles hoped that the mere threat of nuclear weapons would be a sufficient deterrent to the Communists, as the crisis continued the Pentagon made plans for their use if Taiwan itself seemed on the verge of invasion.[49]

Under this British pressure the United States agreed to modify its plans. Dulles assured Makins that when the president asked Congress for authorization to use force to defend Taiwan, he would not specifically make a commitment to Quemoy or the Matsus. The secretary of state said that no promises would be made to the Nationalists, either publicly or in private. However, if an attack on the offshore islands seemed like a prelude to an invasion of Taiwan, then American forces would intervene. Dulles also wanted to make it clear to Eden that the long-term goal of the United States was not to force the Nationalists to give up the offshore islands in the face of a Communist threat, but to have Chiang willingly agree to a redeployment off the islands. The secretary of state believed that the administration had done all it could do to meet London's concerns and hoped the "Oracle" would now proceed.[50] Satisfied by the American compromise, Eden agreed to cooperate on "Oracle," telling Makins that "on balance it is now to our advantage to assist the Administration in keeping to a moderate line."[51]

On January 24, 1955, Eisenhower presented Congress with the Formosa Resolution that would authorize him to order the use of force in Taiwan and in "related localities" if it seemed that Taiwan or the Pescadores were under threat of invasion.[52] Aware that London still harbored concerns about the course of events in the Taiwan Straits, Eisenhower wrote a personal letter to Churchill the next day explaining the American position. The president acknowledged London's fear of a Sino-American war but urged Churchill to see the situation from the American point of view. Eisenhower wrote,

> It is probably difficult for you, in your geographical position, to understand how concerned this country is with the solidarity of the Island Barrier in the Western Pacific. Moreover we are concerned that the psychological effect in the Far East of deserting our friends on Formosa would risk a collapse of Asiatic resistance to the Communists. . . . I am certain there is nothing to be gained . . . by meekness and weakness. . . . But I am sure that the free world is surely building trouble for itself unless it is united in basic purpose, is clear and emphatic in its declared determination to resist all forceful Communist advance, and keeps itself ready to act in a moment's notice if necessary.[53]

Churchill noted, "There is a slightly acid tone about parts of the letter, but, on the whole, it is very good. I agree very strongly about the need to leave the Russians and the Chinese in no doubt as to our determination if pressed too far."[54] Perhaps Eisenhower hoped that Churchill would be more sympathetic to the American position than Eden had so far proven. If that was the case, the president would be disappointed in the long run.

On January 28, 1955, the first step toward implementing "Oracle" finally went forward. New Zealand proposed to the Security Council that it should discuss the hostilities in the Taiwan Straits. On January 31 the Security Council agreed to invite the PRC to participate in the discussion. However, on February 4, 1955, Zhou Enlai rejected this offer. Beijing demanded that the Nationalists be ejected from the UN before it would negotiate with the Security Council.[55] As the UN considered New Zealand's proposal, the State Department, despite Dulles's promise to Makins, informally told Chiang Kai-shek that the United States would defend Quemoy and the Matsus if an attack on them seemed to be a prelude to an invasion of Taiwan itself.[56]

Washington had finally convinced London to launch "Oracle." However, in order to do so it had been necessary for the United States to refrain from a public commitment to the defense of the offshore islands. Eden had succeeded in injecting an element of restraint into American policy. While Churchill agreed with Eisenhower's call to stand firmly against Communism, his government did not think that the offshore islands were the appropriate place to make a stand. The British saw the islands as having no military and economic value and thus believed that their defense was not worth the risk of a general war. Fighting to defend the valuable resources of Malaya made sense; risking a global nuclear war to prop up the morale of Chiang Kai-shek was not reasonable from London's point of view.

CONTINUED DIPLOMACY: FEBRUARY 1955

Although the potential for a peaceful settlement looked bleak after Beijing rejected "Oracle," hopes of a diplomatic solution soon took on a new life. The Soviet Union proposed to the British that an international conference meet to discuss China. Moscow proposed that Britain, India, and the USSR invite the United States, the PRC, France, Burma, Pakistan, Sri Lanka, and Indonesia to the talks.[57]

Eden did not initially accept the Soviet offer. However, he wanted to continue talking to Moscow in order to keep the door open for further negotiations. The foreign secretary suggested to the Americans that if Washington could privately assure Britain that its goal was to get Chiang to evacuate all the offshore islands, then a diplomatic solution would be easier to accomplish. London also wanted to delay pushing "Oracle" to a vote now that it would obviously end in failure because of Beijing's refusal to come to the

UN. Dulles refused to offer London any assurances that Washington wanted the Nationalists to evacuate the offshore islands, claiming that America had retreated as far as it could. The secretary of state believed that the Communist threat to invade Taiwan had to be taken seriously. Dulles asserted that the offshore islands would not be handed over to the PRC under duress. Although the secretary of state wished to continue to bring "Oracle" to a vote, he did agree that this vote could be delayed for a while. Finally, Dulles informed London that the United States would not go to a conference to which Taipei had not been invited.[58]

London urged restraint on the Americans. The British reminded Washington that it would not find any support for a war over the offshore islands among its allies. Eden advised the Americans that as long as their policy on the offshore islands remained vague, the chances for an unwanted war remained high.[59] However, Washington remained firm in its stance that unless a guarantee existed that the offshore islands would not be used as steppingstones for an invasion of Taiwan, American forces might be compelled to assist in their defense.[60]

On February 10, 1955, Eisenhower sent another letter to Churchill outlining America's views on the offshore islands. Eisenhower suggested that one of the prime reasons that the Communists kept up the pressure in the Taiwan Straits was their hope of causing a rift between Washington and London. The president expressed a hope that "nothing is ever going to separate us or destroy our unity in opposing Communist aggression." But pressing his main point, Eisenhower argued that loss of the offshore islands would cause a critical collapse in Nationalist morale. The president believed that if Taiwan fell, the whole Western position in East Asia would be jeopardized. The letter reiterated the American resolve to meet by force any attack on the offshore islands that seemed like a preliminary to an invasion of Taiwan.[61] However, the president failed to outline just how American forces would tell the difference between a localized attack and one meant to create a springboard to reach Taiwan.

Churchill and Eden worked together to craft a reply to Eisenhower. In the message to the president, the British acknowledged that the United States had a responsibility to defend Chiang Kai-shek on Taiwan but urged that Washington should make no promise to the Nationalists to help them hold the offshore islands. Churchill's letter urged Eisenhower to separate the offshore islands, which rightly belonged to Beijing, from the question of Taiwan. The prime minister pointed out that Taiwan itself stood one hundred miles from the mainland and the United States enjoyed naval and air superiority in the area. This would make it impossible for the PLA to launch an amphibious invasion. Alluding to World War II, Churchill reminded Eisenhower, "You and I have already studied, and indeed lived through, such a problem both ways." Rather than encouraging Chiang in his delusions of reconquest, Churchill urged the complete evacuation of the offshore islands. In order to permanently settle the problem, the prime minister suggested that America should reaffirm its commitment to defend Taiwan and the Pescadores, while declaring that the Nationalists would withdraw from the coastal islands with American help within three months. As a means of saving face, Washington could warn that any attempt by Beijing to interfere with the redeployment would be met with overwhelming force.[62]

Churchill and Eden's arguments did not sway Eisenhower. In his reply to Churchill's letter, the president outlined the reasons why he and Dulles would not change their minds. Eisenhower admitted that he would like to see Chiang evacuate the offshore islands. (Indeed Eisenhower had jokingly remarked to a congressional delegation, "Those damned little offshore islands. Sometimes I wish they'd sink."[63]) Despite this view Washington could not force the Nationalists to withdraw. In any event Chiang might decide to fight for the islands even without American aid. Washington believed that a crushing defeat for the Nationalist army would be a disaster for the Western position in East Asia, particularly as the French had now been defeated in Indochina. Eisenhower claimed that the United States had pushed Taipei as far as it could on the matter of the offshore islands. He listed the concessions Taipei had already made: the U.S.-Taiwan treaty did not cover the offshore islands, the Tachens had been evacuated, Chiang had promised not to attack the mainland without American approval, and the Nationalists had supported "Oracle." The president argued that to make further concessions to Beijing would only fuel further aggression, as Munich had encouraged Hitler. Furthermore, the prestige of the United States in Asia would collapse if the Nationalists were abandoned to Beijing. Eisenhower urged London to have faith that America would not blunder into war. He closed by pointedly telling Churchill, "It would surely not be popular in this country if we became involved in possible hostilities on account of Hong Kong or Malaya, which our people look on as 'colonies.' . . . Nevertheless, I do not doubt that if the issue were framed in this way, we would be at your side."[64]

With no convergence of opinion in sight, Dulles and Eden agreed to discuss the matter in person at the SEATO meeting in Bangkok in late February 1955.[65] For the most part the two men rehashed the debate along the same lines as the Eisenhower-Churchill correspondence. Dulles told Eden that it looked increasingly as if the PLA were preparing for an attack. He urged that "Oracle" now be brought to a vote, as even if the USSR vetoed the measure it would focus world attention on the intransigence of the Communists. Eden continued to urge restraint on his American counterpart.[66]

Fearing the worst, the foreign secretary made a bold offer to Beijing while in Bangkok. Eden offered to meet Zhou Enlai in Hong Kong to act as an intermediary between the PRC and the United States.[67] In explaining his plan to Churchill, Eden wrote, "You realize my reluctance to offer to go to Hong Kong. . . . But my conversation with Foster Dulles yesterday evening has convinced me that the situation is grave and urgent action is imperative."[68] In any event, Zhou refused the British offer, insisting that the United States withdraw its forces from Taiwan before any negotiations could begin with Eden.[69]

February ended gloomily as neither Washington nor London would budge from their stance on the offshore islands. The Americans tried to convince the British that the psychological significance of the offshore islands far outweighed their military importance. Eisenhower linked a withdrawal to the appeasement of the Nazis. Churchill and Eden, well known for their public rejection of the appeasement of Hitler, refused to see the situation in this light. They did not believe that a tactical retreat from an untenable position constituted appeasement. To London, the islands were militarily useless and their continued occupation by the Nationalists was a danger to world peace. The containment of Communism in East Asia did not rest on the defense of the offshore islands. Moreover, the British firmly believed that Chiang Kai-shek would be perfectly safe without these isolated outposts.

THE CLIMAX OF THE CRISIS: MARCH 1955

In March, the danger of war seemed to intensify as the United States publicly talked about the possible use of atomic weapons to defend the offshore islands. Eisenhower and Dulles agreed that tactical atomic weapons would be necessary to stop the Nationalist forces from being overrun by a PLA attack. Eisenhower instructed Dulles to make a public statement that nuclear weapons were "interchangeable with . . . conventional weapons" in order to prepare public opinion for their use.[70]

In the House of Commons Eden appealed for peace. On March 8, 1955, he outlined his thoughts on the crisis during a foreign affairs debate. Eden praised the United States for showing restraint so far. He also applauded Beijing for not attacking the offshore islands. The foreign secretary called on Beijing to renounce the use of force to regain Taiwan in exchange for a Nationalist evacuation of the offshore islands and Chiang's pledge not to invade the mainland. Once these steps had been taken, Eden promised that "consideration could then be given internationally . . . to the problem of Chinese representation in the UN and the future status of Formosa."[71]

Unlike his British counterpart, Dulles's idea of pursuing a peaceful solution was exclusively confined to his plan for a UN Security Council resolution. He warned London that the United States might proceed on its own to ask for a vote in the Security Council on "Oracle" if the allies could not agree on concerted action.[72] Eden continued to argue against bringing "Oracle" to a vote. He suggested that the PRC might be goaded into military action if it seemed like a cease-fire would be imposed. In any event, Eden felt sure that the USSR would veto the measure. If that were the case, the United Kingdom had no intention of being "hooked to defend Chiang Kai-shek on Quemoy" for the sake of Western unity. If Washington still demanded some form of UN action, Eden suggested that the Security Council ask Britain, India, and the USSR to investigate the offshore islands problem.[73] Dulles rejected this plan but urged London to cooperate with Moscow and New Delhi to convince Beijing to accept a cease-fire while Washington did the same with the Nationalists.[74]

In Eden's opinion, Dulles's obsession with a cease-fire reflected a misreading of the overall situation. London did not believe that the PRC had any intention of resorting to force to capture Taiwan or even the offshore islands. It served Beijing's purposes to continue the status quo as it could portray the United States as the real threat to peace in East Asia. Eden feared that the Chinese would use the upcoming Bandung Conference of nonaligned states to mobilize Asian political opinion behind their claim to Taiwan.[75] Trying to bring the matter to a head in the Security Council would only make it seem that the United States wanted to secure Chiang's presence on the islands.[76] On March 26, 1955, Dulles reluctantly agreed to postpone voting on "Oracle," caustically writing, "Dear Anthony: I rather expected the Soviets to veto the Resolution but I must confess I did not expect that you would." Dulles warned, however, that the administration expected action on "Oracle" in the near future.[77]

At the end of March the frustration that Washington felt at not being able to get the British to accept its position was revealed in a letter from Eisenhower to Churchill. "Although we seem always to see eye to eye with you when we contemplate any European problem," Eisenhower wrote, "our respective attitudes toward similar problems in the Orient are frequently so dissimilar as to be almost mutually antagonistic. . . . Possibly this fact troubles you and your associates as much as it does us. The conclusion seems inescapable that these differences come about because . . . your . . . government seems to regard Communist aggression in Asia as of little significance to the free world." Eisenhower went on to compare the need to stand up to the Communists to the need to resist the dictators of World War II: "I do believe that all of us must begin to look at some of these unpleasant facts squarely in the face and meet them exactly as our Grand Alliance of the Forties met our enemies and vanquished them." Eisenhower leavened his harsh criticism by expressing his confidence in Churchill's devotion to good Anglo-American relations. He urged Churchill "not to think of this letter as a complaint, or as an effort to prove that we are right or you are wrong. . . . I am interested in one thing and one thing only—how can we and our two governments come closer together in our thinking so as to achieve a better result in matters that are serious and fateful for both our nations?"[78]

The president's message, directed, in any case, to a prime minister near retirement, did not succeed in modifying Britain's determination to pursue its own course with regard to the offshore islands. In mid-April 1955, when the PLA appeared to be building up its forces on the mainland opposite Taiwan, Dulles urged the United Kingdom to issue a statement committing British forces to the defense of Taiwan and the Pescadores as a means of deterring Beijing. Eden, who was by now prime minister, believed that a serious Anglo-American breach over Taiwan would be "a tragic thing." However, while the British were willing to help Washington to seek a peaceful evacuation of the offshore islands, they were unwilling to make a major policy shift such as a guarantee of Taiwan would entail. Such an action would run counter to London's hopes of achieving a modus vivendi with Beijing.[79]

Unexpectedly, at the Bandung Conference, Beijing offered a way out of the crisis. Zhou, claiming that the "Chinese people do not want a war with the United States," offered to begin bilateral cease-fire negotiations with Washington.[80] In a press conference on April 26, 1955, Dulles quickly signaled the administration's willingness to meet with Chinese officials. Dulles stressed that the talks would be limited strictly to a cease-fire, as Washington would discuss nothing else dealing with the Nationalists' fate without a representative from Taipei.[81] The crisis in the Taiwan Straits receded after this exchange. In July 1955, while at the Geneva Summit, Eden advised the Americans to begin the talks with Beijing as soon as possible. On July 25, 1955, the State Department announced that ambassadorial-level talks would begin in August in Geneva.[82] While these talks did not result in a final settlement of the dispute, the immediate danger of a general war had passed.[83]

CONCLUSION

Historians who have studied Anglo-American relations during the First Offshore Islands Crisis have come to different conclusions as to how much London influenced Washington's behavior. Michael Dockrill believes that Britain failed to achieve any of its goals during the crisis. According to Dockrill, the United States did not change any of its basic policies, such as nonrecognition of Beijing. In Dockrill's opinion, the United Kingdom, which depended heavily on the American alliance for security in Europe, "had too much to lose to risk a serious breach with the United States over the Formosa issue." All that London could hope to accomplish was to try to restrain the United States so that it did not start a war with the PRC in the Taiwan Straits.[84] Qiang Zhai's 1994 book, *The Dragon, the Lion, and the Eagle: Chinese/British/American Relations, 1949–58*, agrees with Dockrill's stance that Great Britain was very dependent on Washington and thus often followed the American lead on China policy. He points to Britain's support of America in the Korean War and its failure to push for Beijing's membership in the UN as prime examples of London's deference to Washington. However, Zhai contends that Washington did not always get its way with the British. London's recognition of Beijing in 1950 and the amount of pressure the British put on the United States to moderate its stance on the offshore islands stand out as episodes illustrating London's independence from its American ally.[85] Robert Boardman has portrayed the outcome of the crisis as a compromise between the United States and Great Britain with both nations taking steps toward a two Chinas policy. The United States accepted direct negotiations with Beijing without the presence of the Nationalists. For its part, London had to accept that the United States remained committed to defending Taiwan and the Pescadores and made no attempt to get Washington to change its basic policy toward the Nationalists.[86]

While each of these views have merit, none provides a completely satisfactory analysis of Anglo-American relations in the context of the First Offshore Islands Crisis. On the surface it may have seemed that the United States and Britain compromised their original policies as Boardman suggests. However, more recently available documents show that the United States agreed to meet with Beijing only because the administration believed that it had no other choice if it hoped to avoid war. Eisenhower and Dulles did not want to fight to protect the offshore islands but could not convince Chiang Kai-shek to voluntarily evacuate. Anxious to find a peaceful solution, Washington jumped at the chance to arrange a bilateral cease-fire with the PRC, even at the price of a face-to-face meeting with the Chinese Communists. During the entire course of the crisis, Britain stuck to its original stance that the Nationalists should retreat from the offshore islands. London only agreed to support "Oracle" because it hoped that a cease-fire would be the first step in improving Western relations with Beijing.

Michael Dockrill is undeniably correct in stating that Britain's long-term goal of promoting better Sino-Western relations was not met during or after the crisis in the Taiwan Straits. He points out that London had no success in fundamentally changing Washington's policy toward China. On the other hand, Washington was similarly unsuccessful in altering London's China policy. During the crisis period in 1954–1955, Britain not only stood firmly by its own policy on the offshore islands but also managed to modify American actions. Despite impassioned pleas for Anglo-American unity and dire warnings of a Western collapse in East Asia, Churchill's government resisted Washington's pressure to bring "Oracle" to a vote or to offer a public guarantee to help protect Taiwan. Indeed, the Eisenhower administration had to retreat from its plan to make a public guarantee to defend Quemoy and the Matsus under British pressure. Throughout the crisis the British held to their call for restraint and for a Nationalist surrender of the offshore islands. The continued independence of British policy can be seen as a victory against American pressure to fall in line.

Qiang Zhai's view of the crisis as an example of Britain's determination to follow its own policies is valid. However, his contention that the United Kingdom tended to follow American policy in general is less convincing. Britain's independence from American policy seems more the norm that the exception in terms of China and East Asia. The Korean War appears to have been an anomalous situation. Faced with naked Communist aggression, London joined the American-led defense of South Korea. However, on most other major issues the British had acted contrary to American desires, not the least of which were recognition of the PRC and support for the Geneva Accords on Indochina.

The First Offshore Islands Crisis is a perfect example of Britain's diplomatic independence and continued importance as a global power. Although Churchill and Eden appreciated the depth of American feeling about the offshore islands, and the Nationalist cause in general, they would not abandon their own hopes of improving relations with Beijing and moderating American policy in East Asia. In East Asia, as in Europe and the Middle East, Great Britain showed that its foreign policies were not solely dictated by the importance of placating its American ally. On the contrary, Washington showed that it placed a very high value on its friendship with Britain and would modify its policies to ensure the health of the Anglo-American alliance.

NOTES

1. Robert Boardman, *Britain and the People's Republic of China, 1949–1974* (London, 1976), 24–27; Qiang Zhai, *The Dragon, the Lion, and the Eagle: Chinese/British/American Relations, 1949–58* (Kent, OH, 1994), 44.
2. Zhai, *The Dragon, the Lion, and the Eagle*, 12.
3. Zhai, *The Dragon, the Lion, and the Eagle*, 98–99.
4. Zhai, *The Dragon, the Lion, and the Eagle*, 112, 132.
5. Michael Dockrill, "Britain and the First Chinese Offshore Islands Crisis," *British Foreign Policy, 1945–56*, edited by Michael Dockrill and John Young (New York, 1989), 175–76.

6. Zhai, *The Dragon, the Lion and the Eagle*, 86–88.
7. Zhai, *The Dragon, the Lion and the Eagle*, 146–52.
8. Dockrill, "Offshore Islands Crisis," 173–75.
9. Zhai, *The Dragon, the Lion, and the Eagle*, 157–58.
10. Gordon Chang, *Friends and Enemies: The United States, China, and the Soviet Union, 1948–1972* (Stanford, CA, 1990), 116–18.
11. FRUS 1952–1954 XIV, no. 273, September 4, 1954, Dulles to the State Department.
12. FRUS 1952–1954 XIV, no. 278, September 5, 1954, Dulles to the State Department.
13. FRUS 1952–1954 XIV, no. 281, September 6, 1954, acting secretary of state to Dulles.
14. FRUS 1952–1954 XIV, no. 284, September 8, 1954, Eisenhower to the acting secretary of state.
15. FRUS 1952–1954 XIV, no. 292, September 12, 1954, memorandum by Dulles.
16. Chang, *Friends and Enemies*, 120–21.
17. PRO, FO 371/110231, September 15, 1954, Makins to the Foreign Office.
18. PRO, FO 371/110231, September 16, 1954, Foreign Office minute, Far Eastern Department, "Appendix A."
19. PRO, CAB 128/027, September 17, 1954, cc (54), 60th conclusion.
20. PRO, FO 371/110231, September 17, 1954, record of meeting between Eden and Dulles.
21. FRUS 1952–1954 XIV, no. 300, September 22, 1954, memorandum of conversation between Dulles and Dixon.
22. PRO, FO 371/110231, September 23, 1954, Dixon to the Foreign Office; FRUS 1952–1954 XIV, no. 305, September 27, 1954, Dulles to the State Department.
23. PRO, FO 371/110231, September 30, 1954, Foreign Office to Dixon; FO 371/110231, September 30, 1954, Dixon to the Foreign Office; FO 371/110231, October 1, 1954, Caccia to Dixon.
24. PRO, FO 371/110232, October 2, 1954, Eden to the British UN Delegation.
25. PRO, FO 371/110232, October 4, 1954, British Embassy in Washington, "Record of a Meeting at the State Department."
26. FRUS 1952–1954 XIV, no. 323, October 6, 1954, memorandum of conversation.
27. PRO, FO 371/110233, October 8, 1954, Dixon to the Foreign Office.
28. PRO, FO 371/110233, October 8, 1954, Nutting to Eden.
29. FRUS 1952–1954 XIV, no. 328, October 8, 1954, memorandum of conversation.
30. FRUS 1952–1954 XIV, no. 332, October 9, 1954, memorandum of conversation; PRO, FO 371/110233, October 9, 1954, Makins to the Foreign Office.
31. FRUS 1952–1954 XIV, no. 336, October 10, 1954, memorandum of conversation; PRO, FO 371/110233, October 11, 1954, Foreign Office minute by Allen.
32. PRO, CAB 128/027, October 12, 1954, cc (54), 60th conclusion.
33. Zhai, *The Dragon, the Lion, and the Eagle*, 155–65.
34. Zhai, *The Dragon, the Lion, and the Eagle*, 165–66.
35. PRO, FO 371/110234, October 14, 1954, Makins to the Foreign Office.
36. PRO, FO 371/110234, October 15, 1954, Eden to Makins.

37. PRO, FO 371/110235, October 18, 1954, Makins to the Foreign Office.

38. PRO, FO 371/110238, November 23, 1954, Makins to the Foreign Office.

39. PRO, FO 371/110238, November 24, 1954, Eden to Makins; FO 371/110236, November 27, 1954, Eden to Makins.

40. PRO, FO 371/110236, November 30, 1954, Makins to the Foreign Office.

41. Zhai, *The Dragon, the Lion, and the Eagle*, 166–67.

42. PRO, FO 371/110236, December 1, 1954, Foreign Office to the British Embassy in Washington.

43. PRO, FO 371/110240, December 6, 1954, Makins to the Foreign Office.

44. PRO, FO 371/110240, December 7, 1954, Eden to Makins.

45. PRO, FO 371/110242, December 17, 1954, Eden to the Foreign Office; FO 371/110243, December 20, 1954, Allen to Scott.

46. Chang, *Friends and Enemies*, 121–24.

47. PRO, FO 371/115023, January 20, 1955, Makins to the Foreign Office.

48. PRO, FO 371/115023, January 20, 1955, Eden to Makins.

49. Richard H. Immerman, *John Foster Dulles: Piety, Pragmatism, and Power in U.S. Foreign Policy* (Wilmington, DE, 1999), 130.

50. FRUS 1955–1957 II, no. 26, January 21, 1955, memorandum of the 233rd meeting of the NSC; PRO, FO 371/115024, January 21, 1955, Makins to the Foreign Office.

51. PRO, FO 371/115024, January 22, 1955, Eden to Makins.

52. FRUS 1955–1957 II, pp. 115–119, January 24, 1955, message from the president to Congress.

53. FRUS 1955–1957 II, no. 41, January 25, 1955, Churchill to Eisenhower.

54. Churchill Papers, 2/217, correspondence with Eisenhower, Churchill College, Cambridge University.

55. Dockrill, "Offshore Islands Crisis," 183–84.

56. Zhai, *The Dragon, the Lion, and the Eagle*, 168.

57. PRO, FO 371/115032, February 4, 1955, Hayter to the Foreign Office.

58. FRUS 1955–1957 II, no. 96, February 7, 1955, memorandum of conversation.

59. PRO, FO 371/115033, February 8, 1955, Eden to Makins.

60. PRO, FO 371/115035, February 9, 1955, Makins to the Foreign Office.

61. PRO, PREM 11/879, February 10, 1955, Eisenhower to Churchill.

62. PRO, PREM 11/879, February 15, 1955, Churchill to Eisenhower.

63. Robert Ferrell, ed., *The Diary of James C. Hagerty: Eisenhower in Mid-Course, 1954–55* (Bloomington, IN, 1983), 197.

64. PRO, PREM 11/879, February 19, 1955, Eisenhower to Churchill.

65. FRUS 1955–1957 II, pp. 291–92, February 18, 1955, Aldrich to the State Department.

66. John Foster Dulles to Dwight D. Eisenhower, February 25, 1955, box 4, February 1955 (1), Dulles-Herter series, papers of Dwight D. Eisenhower as president, Eisenhower Library.

67. PRO, FO 371/115039, February 25, 1955, Eden to the Foreign Office.

68. PRO, FO 371/115039, February 25, 1955, Eden to Churchill.

69. PRO 371/115040, March 1, 1955, Trevelyan to the Foreign Office.

70. FRUS 1955–1957 II, no. 141, March 6, 1955, memorandum of conversation; Chang, *Friends and Enemies*, 126–27.

71. PRO, FO 371/115045, March 8, 1955, extract from parliamentary debates.

72. PRO, FO 371/115042, March 9, 1955, Makins to Eden.

73. FRUS 1955–1957 II, no. 152, March 14, 1955, memorandum of conversation.

74. PRO, FO 371/115042, March 16, 1955, Makins to Eden.

75. PRO, FO 371/115042, March 16, 1955, Eden to Makins.

76. FRUS 1955–1957 II, no. 168, March 25, 1955, Eden to Dulles.

77. FRUS 1955–1957 II, no. 171, March 26, 1955, Dulles to Eden.

78. FRUS 1955–1957 II, no. 177, March 29, 1955, Eisenhower to Churchill.

79. FRUS 1955–1957 II, no 208, April 20, 1955, memorandum of conversation; Dockrill, "Offshore Islands Crisis," 187.

80. Dockrill, "Offshore Islands Crisis," 188.

81. FRUS 1955–1957 II, no. 222, April 26, 1955, Dulles press conference.

82. Boardman, *Britain and the People's Republic*, 128–29.

83. Dockrill, "Offshore Islands Crisis," 188–90.

84. Dockrill, "Offshore Islands Crisis," 190–92.

85. Zhai, *The Dragon, the Lion, and the Eagle*, 210–14.

86. Boardman, *Britain and the People's Republic*, 134–35.

Chapter Six

Conclusion

What conclusions can be drawn from the four case studies examined in this book? It seems clear that in the years before the Suez Crisis of late 1956, Great Britain retained its position as a world power. Some proof of this is self-evident, as the power and size of Britain's economy and military compared favorably to all other nations except the two superpowers. In addition, the British Empire and Commonwealth controlled important bases around the globe. However, as David Reynolds has pointed out, possession of the means and outward signs of global power are not the same as exercising global power.[1] Evidence of the reality of Britain's power can be seen in the fact that it could pursue foreign policy goals that were at odds with those of its gargantuan American ally. This is not to say that Britain gave limited importance to Anglo-American relations. In fact, Great Britain placed the support of the United States at the center of its plan to retain its empire as well as protect Western Europe from the Soviet Union. But Britain did not place its own policies, designed to defend its status as a global power, in subordination to the American plans for containing Communism. In the context of the early Cold War, London's efforts to hold onto its far-flung colonies and bases in order to maintain its own national power attracted American support because the British Empire remained a formidable shield against Communism in many areas of the globe. Churchill's government proved to be adept at exploiting this reality.

Churchill's drive for an East-West summit reveals two facts: Britain could still make a contribution to the nature of the relations between the Soviet Union and the West by promoting détente, and Churchill was not afraid to try to force the Eisenhower administration to go along with his scheme for promoting better East-West relations. This case study is unique in that it represents not a disagreement between the British and American governments as much as it represents a disagreement between Churchill and the combined American and British opponents of his summit plan. However, the personal nature of the prime minister's summit plan demonstrates that Churchill himself, despite his reverence for the "special relationship," was willing to try to exploit the importance of the British to the Americans as well as his personal relationship with Eisenhower. If Churchill had successfully concluded a meeting with the Soviet leadership, the Eisenhower administration would have been under intense public pressure to continue détente. Undoubtedly, this is what Churchill counted on when he planned his Anglo-Soviet summit: giving up on his idea only when the Soviets seemed more intent on disrupting West German rearmament than on real negotiations.

In Iraq, Great Britain exploited the American obsession with containment to prop up its own faltering influence over Baghdad. Under pressure from London, the United States refused to replace the British as the chief weapons supplier to Iraq. The American decision was based in large measure on the fact that Britain had a long-standing relationship with the Iraqi government and military that would have been costly to replicate. From the Eisenhower administration's point of view, Iraq's strategic importance to the West could best be utilized by having Baghdad remain a British client. Of course, Britain's success in maintaining its close relationship with Iraq was short-lived. And while this points to the underlying weakness of Britain, neither London nor Washington saw the rapid decline of the British position in the Middle East as a real possibility in the early 1950s.

In the struggle over the Buraimi Oasis the continuation of British power is clearly demonstrated. While Churchill and Eden were willing to try to reach a compromise with Saudi Arabia in deference to the Saudi-American relationship, London had limits to how far it would bend. To London, standing up to the Saudis in order to preserve British prestige in the Middle East and defend the oil of the Persian Gulf proved more important than placating the United States. While it was under Eden's premiership that the Saudis were forcibly ejected from the oasis, Churchill had also supported a hard line with Riyadh. Faced with a choice between supporting the British or the Saudis, the United States tried to mediate but ultimately backed the British arbitration proposal and took no action to punish Britain when it withdrew from negotiations and occupied the disputed territory in the name of its Gulf allies. To Washington, the value of its alliance with Great Britain outweighed the risk to the Saudi-American friendship and Aramco's oil concession.

Moving lastly to East Asia, the First Offshore Islands Crisis provides further evidence of the continued global importance of the British Empire. The crisis surrounding the small Nationalist-held islands highlighted the differences between British and American policies over China and the best method of containing Communism in East Asia. While not anxious for war, the Eisenhower administration pursued a hard line with the People's Republic of China and feared that failure to adequately support Chiang Kai-shek would only reward Communist aggression in Asia. Despite intense American pressure to fall in line with their policy, the British government remained committed to its plan of promoting a wide-ranging peaceful settlement to the Cold War in East Asia to help safeguard its valuable colonial possessions in the region. In the end, Great Britain moderated the American stance on the offshore islands and forestalled a public commitment by the Eisenhower administration to help the Nationalists defend the islands. While neither government changed its basic policy in East Asia as a result of the crisis, Washington demonstrated that it felt compelled to have British support to take an unambiguously aggressive stance in the Taiwan Straits and London felt confident that it could rebuff American pleas for public support for their position. Once again Great Britain showed that it could pursue its own foreign policy goals in the face of conflicting American aims.

The diplomatic incidents examined in this book also help to answer the related question of the role that the United States played in Britain's eventual decline as a world power. The historiography on the issue is divided, with some historians placing more of the blame for British decline on the United States than others. A prominent proponent of the idea that the American alliance was disastrous for Great Britain is John Charmley, who argues that Churchill's obsession with the "special relationship" strained Britain's resources, provided no benefits to the British, and simply paved the way for Washington to force London into the role of junior partner while enhancing American global power.[2]

Unlike Charmley, who portrays the United States as actively seeking to replace the British Empire with a new American hegemony, D. C. Watt contends that during the Eisenhower years American policies inadvertently damaged the British Empire and therefore forced the United States to reluctantly fill the void left by the retreat of British power. The United States aided in the dissolution of the British Empire by supporting colonial nationalism not because of any desire to supplant Britain, but because of a misguided belief that the nationalist movements of the developing world could be harnessed to the West if old-style European imperialism could be abolished.[3]

Other scholars believe that the United States had only a limited role in diminishing British power. In an examination of the American role in the collapse of the British Empire, Wm. Roger Louis contends that American anticolonialism was always subordinated to the containment of the Soviet Union and that it did not make a major contribution to the decline of Great Britain. While American pressure on the British to create postimperial relationships in the developing world may have sped up the British retreat, the British Empire came to an end because of growing colonial nationalism and the economic weakness of Great Britain.[4] David Reynolds concurs with Louis's conclusion that the United States only pushed the British "faster down the slippery slope" toward imperial decline without being a real cause of that decline.[5]

The evidence examined in this study supports this latter view that American foreign policies were not a major factor in British decline. The United States placed too much value on Britain's position as a global partner in containment to actively seek to undermine its empire. While it is true that the growing American influence in the Middle East caused some problems, and a great deal of concern, for Great Britain, London sought a limited level of American interest in the region to reduce its own defense expenditures. America cannot be blamed for the increase in nationalism in the developing world and the economic weakness of London, which ultimately made the retention of the empire an impossible goal.

While the sun was rapidly setting on the British Empire by the end of the 1950s, the decade after the Second World War saw a resilient and still very powerful Britain making a determined, if ultimately vain, effort to preserve its role as a world power. The relations between the governments of Winston Churchill and Dwight Eisenhower demonstrate that, at least before the Suez Crisis, Great Britain was not simply America's junior partner in containment but an international power capable of pursuing its own goals and defending its own interests.

NOTES

1. David Reynolds, *Britannia Overruled: British Policy and World Power in the Twentieth Century* (New York, 2000), 4–5.
2. John Charmley, *Churchill's Grand Alliance: The Anglo-American Special Relationship, 1940–57* (New York, 1995), 356–61.
3. D. C. Watt, "Demythologizing the Eisenhower Era," in *The 'Special Relationship': Anglo-American Relations Since 1945*, ed. Wm. Roger Louis and Bull Headly (Oxford, 1986), 73–74, 78–83.
4. Wm. Roger Louis, "American Anti-Colonialism and the Dissolution of the British Empire," in *The "Special Relationship': Anglo-American Relations Since 1945*, edited by Wm. Roger Louis and Headly Bull (Oxford, 1986), 280–83.
5. David Reynolds, "Rethinking Anglo-American Relations," *International Affairs* 65, no. 1 (Winter 1985/86): 93.

Bibliography

ARCHIVES AND PUBLISHED DOCUMENTS

Public Record Office, Kew, UK
Papers of Winston Churchill, Churchill College, Cambridge University
National Archives, College Park, Maryland
Eisenhower Library, Abilene, Kansas
Papers of John Foster Dulles, Mudd Library, Princeton University
Foreign Relations of the United States Series (FRUS)

MEMOIRS AND PUBLISHED PAPERS

Butler, R. A., *The Art of the Possible: Memoirs of Lord Butler*, London: Gambit, 1971.

Colville, John, *The Fringes of Power: 10 Downing Street Diaries, 1939–1955*, New York: W. W. Norton & Company, 1985.

Eden, Anthony, *Full Circle*, Boston: Houghton Mifflin, 1960.

Eisenhower, Dwight, *Mandate for Change, 1953–56*, New York: Doubleday & Company, 1963.

Ferrell, Robert, editor, *The Diary of James C. Hagerty: Eisenhower in Mid-course, 1954–55*, Bloomington: Indiana University Press, 1983.

Galambos, Louis, and Van Ee, Duan, editors, *The Papers of Dwight David Eisenhower—The Presidency: The Middle Way*, Baltimore: Johns Hopkins University Press, 1996.

Gallman, Waldermar, *Iraq Under General Nuri: My Recollections of Nuri al-Said, 1954–1958*, Baltimore: Johns Hopkins University Press, 1964.

Griffith, Robert, editor, *Ike's Letter's to a Friend, 1941–1958*, Lawrence: University Press of Kansas, 1984.

Shuckburgh, Evelyn, *Descent to Suez: Diaries, 1951–56*, New York: W. W. Norton & Company, 1986.

Wilson, Charles (Lord Moran), *Churchill: Taken from the Diaries of Lord Moran, The Struggle for Survival, 1940–1965*, Boston: Houghton Mifflin, 1966.

GENERAL WORKS

Ambrose, Stephen, *Eisenhower: Volume Two, The President*, New York: Simon & Schuster, 1984.

Anderson, Irvine, *ARAMCO, the United States, and Saudi Arabia: A Study in the Dynamics of Foreign Oil Policy, 1933–1950*, Princeton, NJ: Princeton University Press, 1981.

Bartlett, C. J., *"The Special Relationship": A Political History of Anglo-American Relations Since 1945*, New York: Longman, 1992.

Bischof, Gunter, and Ambrose, Stephen, editors, *Eisenhower: A Centenary Assessment*, Baton Rouge: Louisiana State University Press, 1995.

Boardman, Robert, *Britain and the People's Republic of China, 1949–1974*, London: Macmillan, 1976.

Bowie, Robert, and Richard Immerman, *Waging Peace: How Eisenhower Shaped an Enduring Cold War Strategy*, New York: Oxford University Press, 1998.

Brands Jr., H. W., *Cold Warriors: Eisenhower's Generation and American Foreign Policy*, New York: Columbia University Press, 1988.

Cain, P. J., and Hopkins, A. G., *British Imperialism: Crisis and Deconstruction, 1914–1990*, New York: Longman, 1993.

Callahan, Raymond, *Churchill's Retreat from Empire*, Wilmington, DE: Scholarly Resources, 1984.

Chalmers, Malcolm, *Paying for Defense: Military Spending and British Decline*, London: Pluto Press, 1985.

Chang, Gordon, *Friends and Enemies: The United States, China, and the Soviet Union, 1948–1972*, Stanford, CA: Stanford University Press, 1990.

Charmley, John, *Churchill's Grand Alliance: The Anglo-American Special Relationship, 1940–57*, New York: Harcourt, Brace & Company, 1995.

Citino, Nathan, *From Arab Nationalism to OPEC: Eisenhower, King Saud and the Making of U.S.-Saudi Relations*, Indianapolis: Indiana University Press, 2002.

Darwin, John, *Britain and Decolonization: The Retreat from Empire in the Postwar World*, New York: Palgrave Macmillan, 1988.

Devereaux, David, *The Formulation of British Defense Policy Towards the Middle East, 1948–1956*, New York: Palgrave Macmillan, 1990.

Dietl, Gulshan, *The Dulles Era: America Enters West Asia*, New Delhi: Lancer International, 1986.

Dimbleby, David, and Reynolds, David, *An Ocean Apart: The Relationship Between Britain and American in the Twentieth Century*, New York: Vintage, 1988.

Divine, Robert, *Eisenhower and the Cold War*, New York: Oxford University Press, 1981.

Dockrill, Michael, *British Defense Since 1945*, New York: Blackwell Publishers, 1988.

Dockrill, Michael, and Young, John, editors, *British Foreign Policy, 1945–56*, New York: Palgrave Macmillan, 1989.

Elliot, Matthew, *Independent Iraq: The Monarchy and British Influence, 1941–58*, New York: Tauris Academic Studies, 1996.

Ewald Jr., William, *Eisenhower the President: Crucial Days, 1951–60*, Englewood Cliffs, NJ: Prentice Hall, 1981.

Fraser, T. G., *The USA and the Middle East Since WWII*, New York: Macmillan, 1989.

Freiberger, Steven, *Dawn Over Suez: The Rise of American Power in the Middle East, 1953–1957*, Chicago: Ivan R. Dee Publishers, 1992.

Gaddis, John L., *Strategies of Containment: A Critical Appraisal of Postwar American National Security Policy*, New York: Oxford University Press, 1982.

Gallagher, John, *The Decline, Revival, and Fall of the British Empire*, New York: Cambridge University Press, 1982.

Gilbert, Martin, *Winston S. Churchill: Volume VIII, "Never Despair, 1945–65,"* Boston: Houghton Mifflin, 1988.

Hahn, Peter, *The United States, Great Britain, and Egypt, 1945–1956: Strategy and Diplomacy in the Early Cold War*, Chapel Hill: University of North Carolina Press, 1991.

Hathaway, Robert, *Great Britain and the United States: Special Relations Since World War II*, Boston: G. K. Hall & Company, 1990.

Holden, David, and Jones, Richard, *The House of Saud: The Rise and Rule of the Most Powerful Dynasty in the Arab World*, New York: Holt Reinhart & Winston, 1981.

Hollowell, Jonathan, editor, *Twentieth Century Anglo-American Relations*, New York: Palgrave Macmillan, 2001.

Humes, James C., *Eisenhower and Churchill: The Partnership that Saved the World*, Roseville, CA: Prima Lifestyles, 2001.

Immerman, Richard H., *John Foster Dulles: Piety, Pragmatism, and Power in U.S. Foreign Policy*, Wilmington, DE: Scholarly Resources, 1999.

——, *John Foster Dulles and the Diplomacy of the Cold War*, Princeton, NJ: Princeton University Press, 1990.

James, Robert R., *Anthony Eden*, New York: McGraw-Hill, 1986.

Kennedy, Paul, *The Rise and Fall of the Great Powers: Economic Change and Military Conflict from 1500 to 2000*, New York: Random House, 1987.

Larres, Klaus, *Churchill's Cold War: The Politics of Personal Diplomacy*, New York: Yale University Press, 2002.

Louis, Wm. Roger, *The British Empire in the Middle East, 1945–51: Arab Nationalism, the United States, and Postwar Imperialism*, Oxford: Oxford University Press, 1984.

Louis, Wm. Roger, and Bull, Headly, editors, *The 'Special Relationship': Anglo-American Relations Since 1945*, Oxford: Oxford University Press, 1986.

Marks III, Frederick, *Power and Peace: The Diplomacy of John Foster Dulles*, Westport, CT: Praeger, 1993.

Marr, Phebe, *The Modern History of Iraq*, Boulder, CO: Westview Press, 1985.

Melanson, Richard, and Mayers, David, editors, *Reevaluating Eisenhower: American Foreign Policy in the 1950s*, Chicago: University of Illinois Press, 1987.

Monroe, Elizabeth, *Britain's Moment in the Middle East, 1914–1971*, Baltimore: Johns Hopkins University Press, 1981.

Moran, Lord, *Churchill: Taken from the Diaries of Lord Moran, The Struggle for Survival, 1940–1965*, Boston: Houghton Mifflin, 1966.

Orde, Anne, *The Eclipse of Great Britain: The United States and Imperial Decline, 1895–1956*, New York: Palgrave Macmillan, 1996.

Ovendale, Ritchie, *Britain, the United States, and the Transfer of Power in the Middle East, 1945–1962*, New York: Leicester University Press, 1996.

Pach Jr., Chester, and Richardson, Elmo, *The Presidency of Dwight D. Eisenhower*, Lawrence: University Press of Kansas, 1991.

Paterson, Thomas G., *On Every Front: The Making and Unmaking of the Cold War*, New York: W. W. Norton & Company, 1992.

Petersen, Tore, *The Middle East between the Great Powers: Anglo-American Conflict and Cooperation, 1952–7*, New York: Palgrave Macmillan, 2000.

——, "Anglo-American Rivalry in the Middle East: The Struggle for the Buraimi Oasis, 1952–57," *International History Review* 14, February 1992.

Reynolds, David, *Britannia Overruled: British Policy and World Power in the Twentieth Century*, New York: Longman, 2000.

——, "Rethinking Anglo-American Relations," *International Affairs* 65, no. 1, Winter 1988/89.

——, "A 'Special Relationship'? America, Britain and the International Order Since the Second World War," *International Affairs* 62, no. 1, Winter 1985/86.

Rothwell, V. H., *Anthony Eden: A Political Biography*, Manchester, UK: Manchester University Press, 1992.

Sanders, David, *Losing an Empire, Finding a Role: An Introduction to British Foreign Policy since 1945*, New York: Palgrave Macmillan, 1989.

Seldon, Anthony, *Churchill's Indian Summer: The Conservative Government, 1951–1955*, London: Hodder & Stoughton, 1981.

Stassen, Harold, and Marshall Houts, *Eisenhower: Turning the World Towards Peace*, St. Paul, MN: Merrill/Mangus Publishing Company, 1990.

Watt, D. Cameron, *Succeeding John Bull: America in Britain's Place, 1900–1975*, New York: University of Cambridge Press, 1984.

Young, John, *Winston Churchill's Last Campaign: Britain and the Cold War, 1951–55*, New York: Oxford University Press, 1996.

——, editor, *The Foreign Policy of Churchill's Peacetime Administration, 1951–55*, Worcester: Leicester University Press, 1988.

Zhai, Qiang, *The Dragon, the Lion, and the Eagle: Chinese/British/American Relations, 1949–58*, Kent, OH: Kent State University Press, 1994.

Index

About the Author

Daniel C. Williamson has been Assistant Professor of History at the University of Hartford's Hillyer College since 2001. He received a Ph.D. in Modern European History from the University of Connecticut, a master's degree from Villanova University, and a bachelor's degree from Fairfield University. He resides in Manchester, Connecticut, with his wife Cathy and their son Conor.

18288059R00081

Made in the USA
Lexington, KY
25 October 2012